Trading Stocks Using Classical Chart Patterns

A Complete Tactical & Psychological Guide
for Beginners and Experienced Traders

Over <u>100</u> chart examples
Detailed entry and exit strategies
Emphasis on managing risk
The mental game

BRIAN B. KIM

ISBN-10: 0990908909
ISBN-13: 978-0-9909089-0-6

For my family.

CONTENTS

PART I - A FRIENDLY INTRODUCTION 1

    CHAPTER 1 Our Goal...3

    CHAPTER 2 Trading vs. Investing vs. Gambling........................9

    CHAPTER 3 Emotional Detachment and
                Acknowledging Our Limitations 12

    CHAPTER 4 Basic Trading Tools..21

PART II - CLASSICAL CHART PATTERNS............................25

    CHAPTER 5 Head & Shoulders Top 27

    CHAPTER 6 Head & Shoulders Bottom 40

    CHAPTER 7 Continuation H&S Bottom 61

    CHAPTER 8 Rectangle...67

    CHAPTER 9 Ascending Triangle 75

    CHAPTER 10 Descending Triangle..91

    CHAPTER 11 Symmetrical Triangle...96

    CHAPTER 12 Continuation Pennant (Small Triangle)................133

    CHAPTER 13 Ascending Wedge 141

    CHAPTER 14 Descending Wedge...145

    CHAPTER 15 Flags and Channels..155

    CHAPTER 16 H&S Top Failure 171

    CHAPTER 17 Double Bottom 183

    CHAPTER 18 Horn Bottom 186

    CHAPTER 19 Diamond...190

    CHAPTER 20 Second and Third Effort....................................193

    CHAPTER 21 Support and Resistance......................................195

    CHAPTER 22 Pattern within a Pattern....................................203

    CHAPTER 23 Pattern Failures and Mutations..........................214

    CHAPTER 24 Do Not Gamble on Earnings Reports.................225

    CHAPTER 25 Being Out of Position: Not Trading
    No Matter How Promising the Set-Up and Breakout.............228

CHAPTER 26   Taking Profits 235
CHAPTER 27   Why We Must Diversify Our Trades 242
CHAPTER 28   The Trader's Routine: Continuous
Patience and Diligence 245
CHAPTER 29   Trading the Market Indexes, and A Lesson in
Stubbornness 268
CHAPTER 30   50-day and 200-day Simple Moving Averages 279

PART III - CONCLUSION 283
CHAPTER 31   Life and Trading 285
CHAPTER 32   Suggested Reading 287

ABOUT THE AUTHOR 289
DISCLAIMER 291

PART I

A FRIENDLY INTRODUCTION

CHAPTER 1
Our Goal

This book teaches you how to trade stocks using classical chart patterns and related principles.

<u>Clarity and usefulness</u>

I strived to write a book that covers the classical-charting approach to trading in an accessible and comprehensive manner. This book gives beginners enough information to decide for themselves whether trading in general and classical charting in particular fit their interest, temperament, and style. My goal is similar if you are an experienced trader who wants to learn more about classical charting. I tried to give you enough information so you can decide whether to use classical charting in your trading.

My focus was on clarity and thoroughness. My experience with most books on stock trading has been one of frustration and confusion. While they contained nuggets of wisdom and some practical advice, most books did not describe the author's trading approach in enough detail for readers to carefully try that approach for themselves.

This shortcoming is understandable. Writing clearly is difficult. And I'm certain that some readers will wish that I had explained some parts of this book better or in a different way. Despite the challenges of written communication, I think I have clearly conveyed enough information for readers to learn classical charting.

You will find that certain themes, reminders, and cautions are repeated quite often throughout the book. It would be too easy to justify repetitive writing on necessity, but, this time, I will use this excuse. There are many approaches to trading, but there are relatively few principles that are most important for long-term success as a trader. I tried to emphasize these timeless truths in different contexts and situations for maximum retention and awareness.

Trading is speculating

Before moving on, let's make sure we understand that stock trading is speculating. Even to me, an enthusiastic student of the financial markets with significant trading experience, speculation at times seems the opposite of thrift, hard work, patience, and all things that build anything worthwhile. Speculation seems nothing more than a doomed get-rich-quick scheme based on greed, impatience, and laziness.

This characterization, unfortunately, accurately describes speculation as done by many people. It is an especially accurate description of my early trading and it will always reflect the truth when we deviate from good practices and forget the fundamentals, including controlling our emotions and being patient.

It is obvious and true that there is no easy road to wealth in the stock market or anywhere else. I don't say this to be condescending. When I started to trade and experienced some beginner's luck, I suspected trading could be the easy road to wealth. I was wrong. But I learned that trading can be a worthy intellectual and financial endeavor if we accept the fact that good trading requires as much discipline and resilience as anything worth accomplishing. If we try to wish away this truth, we will find that trading is a most effective way to lose money. Again, informed trading that maximizes our chances of success is built on methodical risk management, continuous patience, and never-ending diligence. There is no other way, and we should not want it any other way.

Informed speculation should meet the following three requirements:

- A systematic approach that is understandable and repeatable.
- A systematic approach that allows a trader to be profitable overall despite having more losing than winning trades.

- A systematic approach that stresses limiting losses, not making money, as the most important priority.

I believe carefully applying classical charting principles meets these requirements. This book applies those principles and where productive adds to them with these requirements in mind.

Classical Charting and Technical Analysis

I use solely classical charting as a trader because it provides a simple yet versatile and fascinating foundation on which to trade stocks. A classical chartist trades geometric patterns such as triangles, rectangles, wedges, and flags formed by price charts.

Classical charting is a branch of technical analysis. Technical analysis is a fancy phrase for using the price of stocks, or any freely-traded financial instrument such as bonds and futures, to make trading and investment decisions. Some traders use price and many indicators, which are themselves based on price. I don't use any indicators except for the occasional reference to moving averages. We will learn about moving averages in Chapter 30.

I wrote this book to be as clear, practical, and self-contained as possible to everyone who has a passing interest in trading. Despite this nuts-and-bolts approach, I believe that experienced traders can benefit from this book. Learning is a never-ending process. Many of the most important truths and insights are the most basic and yet easy to forget. Learning is as much about retaining and reminding ourselves of old truths as learning new knowledge.

All chart patterns discussed in this book are applications of classical charting principles that were explained by Richard Schabacker in *Technical Analysis and Stock Market Profits*, published in 1932, and Robert D. Edwards & John Magee, co-authors of *Technical Analysis of Stock Trends*, published in 1948.

Some readers may disagree with my application of classical charting principles. That is fine. There is room for disagreement when interpreting chart patterns. Classical chartists have different trading styles utilizing different entries, timeframes, profit-taking methods, and risk tolerances. What is most important, and what is not debatable, is managing our risk and limiting our losses. Whatever our interpretation of a chart pattern, our priority is managing risk rather than making money.

The charts in this book

[T]here is nothing new under the sun.

Ecclesiastes 1:9

My impression when I read Schabacker and Edwards & Magee's foundational works on classical charting was one of fascination but also disbelief. Sure, those simple and elegant price patterns may have formed in stock charts back in the 1930s, 1940s, 1950s, 1960s, and maybe even the 1970s and 1980s, but surely such geometric patterns are no longer found in today's ultra-sophisticated markets? I doubted, despite my respect for Schabacker, Edwards, and Magee for writing an interesting analysis of stock prices, whether books written decades ago could be relevant today.

My doubts were reasonable but I found that the principles explained in the classic texts continue to be very useful. The fact that **this book contains almost 100 unique chart patterns that formed in the U.S. stock market just in the past couple of years** is proof of the continuing power of classical charting. And I did not include every pattern that I found. Also, many more tradable classical patterns developed in every freely-traded financial instrument, including bonds, commodities, precious metals, and foreign stocks. The financial markets have been forming classical patterns for a long time and will continue to do so.

Just because a chart is included in this book does not mean I traded it. I traded many of the patterns in this book but it would have been impractical and unwise for me to have tried to trade all of them.

When we look at the charts, we must not get impatient and decide to start trading the next day. This caution applies especially to beginners. We must first study. The market is not going anywhere.

This book represents an important fact that all traders must remember but tend to forget: **there will always be many more great trading opportunities**. It is crucial to remind ourselves of this fact because we will experience losing streaks and become frustrated. When we are emotionally and financially down, we are more likely to do foolish things, such as making large bets that place all or most of our trading capital at risk in a desperate bid to make up our losses. It is during challenging times that it is most important to maintain composure and exercise strict risk management. It will be easier for us to maintain our discipline and calm if we truly believe and know that there will be many more chart set-ups to come.

If, instead, we get frustrated because we think we have "missed all the good trading opportunities," then we will try to force something in unfavorable market conditions. Knowing that there will always be more opportunities helps us persevere through losing streaks. And we will have losing streaks even if we trade only ideal setups.

Again, prices of financial instruments have been forming classical chart patterns for many years, and they will continue to do so. Beginners may have a more difficult time accepting this fact because they are eager to start trading and do not want to miss out on any "once-in-a-lifetime" trade setups that will make them rich overnight. We must realize that we will not get rich overnight. We must not think about how a single trade can make us. Instead, our goal is to patiently and methodically build our experience and capital.

The more I trade, the more I believe that surviving and preserving my trading capital, not making money, is my first and only goal as a trader. If we can hang around, then we will always have the opportunity to swing at very favorable trade setups. And they will come.

CHAPTER 2
Trading vs. Investing vs. Gambling

[I]n an astonishingly large proportion of the trading in common stocks,
those engaged therein don't appear to know – in polite terms – one part of
their anatomy from another.

Benjamin Graham

This book explains the classical-charting approach to trading stocks. But
what is trading?

One way to understand trading is to discuss what it is not. We can
compare trading to other activities such as picking individual stocks, using
low-cost stock index funds, and gambling in stocks based on, say, hunches
or tips from a neighbor.

Let's first define investing. In my opinion, for the vast majority of
people looking to put some of their savings in stocks, investing should
mean buying shares in a low-cost index mutual fund that tracks the entire
stock market and staying invested for at least 15 to 20 years, and preferably
20 to 30 years and more. If we were to stay invested in low-cost index funds
for decades, we are likely to do better than most market participants,
including fancy hedge funds and other professional asset managers. Here is
where human nature comes in. I suspect many of us do not like the "most"
qualifier to this otherwise compelling proposition. Rather than just doing
better than most people, we want to beat almost everyone. So we decide to
look for ways to beat the market.

Can we beat the market by picking stocks by ourselves or by buying shares in an actively-managed mutual fund run by professional stock pickers? Individual stock selection can be investing, but can easily become gambling. Why? Because it is very difficult to beat the market picking individual stocks and trying to do so often produces poor, and even disastrous, results.

Wait a second, what about Warren Buffett? Let's say that Warren Buffett's incredible long-term record is indeed based on real skill and not mostly extraordinary luck. By the way, I don't think Mr. Buffett's record is all luck despite the fact that I'm sure he would agree that, as with anything in life, luck can play a significant role. Consider the following. Let's say that Warren Buffett and 100 more extraordinarily skilled stock pickers, out of tens of thousands, have beaten by a meaningful margin the stock market's long-run performance over 20 to 30 years or more. Nobody could know 20 or 30 years ago which stock pickers would do well. Only those investors lucky enough to have picked and stayed with the chosen few would beat the market. That is, even if it is possible to beat the market, it is not likely we will find the very few stock pickers who will.

We don't have to believe that it is essentially impossible to beat the market. I think, however, it is important to acknowledge the difficulty of doing so. Also, it is good to know that low-cost index funds are a very useful investment tool.

Our next question may be: if most people who want to get into stocks should use low-cost index funds, then does that mean trading is nothing more than reckless and risky gambling?

Every form of financial activity, from starting a business to buying a house, carries risk. Even if we invest in index funds, we will lose money if the stock market remains depressed for years and we are unable to stay invested and sell after a market decline. As with investing, trading can easily slide into gambling. The difference between informed trading and gambling lies in the degree and manageability of risk.

I differentiate trading from outright gambling on the basis of the following two factors.

First, skilled traders know that they are speculating. If we trade stocks, then we are speculating rather than investing. Never think otherwise. Traders know and acknowledge the risks. Gamblers, in contrast, are often under the illusion that they are engaging in a relatively safe investment activity when in fact they are just praying for a miracle.

Second, skilled traders, because they know they are speculating, minimize their losses on losing trades so that they can be profitable overall even if most of their trades are losers. One $100 winner makes up for many $10 losers. Uncompromising, unsentimental, and cold-hearted management of risk is the trader's top, and really the only, priority. If we limit our losses and keep our trading capital intact, then we can stay in the game. And when we are in the game, we will always find new opportunities in the markets.

So trading, properly done, is neither investing nor gambling. The possibility of uncompromising risk control, which we must implement ourselves, and the potential for profits is why I use a portion of my savings to trade the financial markets using classical charting principles. If I did not believe I had a reasonable opportunity to match and perhaps beat the market as a classical chartist, then I would put all of my savings into savings accounts and low-cost stock index funds. If, after studying this book, we do not think that classical charting gives us an intellectual framework to trade stocks while effectively managing risk, then we should not become classical chartists. We should not risk even a small part of our savings in a trading or any endeavor that we do not believe in. There is no law that requires us to be in stocks in any way. We don't even have to invest in index funds. **We don't have to prove anything to anyone in the financial markets.** We should consider becoming a classical chartist only after we have studied the markets and carefully considered the potential risks and rewards. We should take our time. The market will always be there.

CHAPTER 3

Emotional Detachment and Acknowledging Our Limitations

Survival is the only road to riches.

Peter Bernstein

We are often taught, wrongly, to avoid failure at all cost

This chapter, in my very immodest opinion, is the most important chapter in the book.

Discussing the distinction between trading and investing and gambling highlights the most important foundation of this book and for traders: the utmost importance of risk management by limiting our losses and keeping our trading capital intact.

If risk management is so important, then why do so many traders fail to manage risk and suffer big and sometimes irreversible losses?

Because we are reluctant to admit that we are wrong. We live in a competitive world where failure is not celebrated. Traders think that honoring their stops and getting out of a trade at a relatively small loss, repeatedly, means they are admitting, repeatedly, to the world that they are life failures. So we refuse to honor our stops and fail to cut our losses by exiting our position. Instead, we stay in until "we break even." We don't want to admit failure on a trade because we are smart and smart people don't lose, especially money. Yet trading using classical charting principles almost guarantees that we will have more losing trades than winning trades.

The point is not to have more winning trades than losing trades. The point is to have several $100 winners swamp many more $10 losers.

In short, we have to be willing to fail, and fail often. If we think about it, we cannot accomplish anything worthwhile in life without being open to failure. Let me stress the following: I am not saying that we have to risk financial ruin to be a successful trader. Quite the contrary. As I have said and will repeat many times throughout the book, traders' first and only priority is financial survival by keeping their trading capital intact through even lengthy losing streaks to be able to bet on advantageous trade set-ups after gaining experience. I repeat: I do not mean bankruptcy when I say a trader must be willing to fail. Successful trading is about being wrong and losing money on many trades and yet being profitable overall because the losses are only a small fraction of our capital.

<u>We may not reach our goal – and that is fine</u>

In addition to expecting to lose on most trades, I think it is very important for traders to acknowledge the possibility that we might not make it as traders. Unless we acknowledge the possibility of failure, we will be so caught up in "making it" and getting rich as traders that it will be impossible to trade well. How can we trade with a clear mind and a laser-like focus on honoring our stops, limiting our losses, and acknowledging losing trades day after day if we tell ourselves that our life and our self-worth depend on every trade? That is too much pressure for anyone.

This destructive potential applies to everything in life. It is impossible to succeed in anything worth accomplishing if we are afraid of failing because we will be too afraid to try or try half-heartedly and timidly.

Don't get me wrong. Trying our best is a good thing. But thinking that our life and our self-worth depend on succeeding as a trader or anything else is a different thing and harmful.

There is nothing wrong with learning about the markets, gaining experience in the markets with minimal loss in savings, and deciding our interests lie elsewhere. If you find the financial markets to be as fascinating as I do, then by all means apply yourself diligently and with purpose to become an investor, trader, or whatever kind of market participant you wish to be. But do not let the markets become a destructive obsession. There are so many more things in life that are far more important.

Diversify financially

So how do we avoid becoming dangerously obsessed with the markets? How can we push ourselves to follow a strict risk-management process that gets us out quickly from losing trades? How can we avoid thinking that our livelihood, life savings, and self-worth depend on the next trade being profitable?

One way is to not have all of our eggs in one basket. We should trade with only a portion of our savings.

Another way is to have some income, whether a part-time or full-time job or our own business. Anything will do. There is dignity in all labor. Making money outside of trading will increase our chances of trading well. Why?

First, the money we earn will be a source of psychological comfort and strength. We will not be so dependent on trading profits to pay our bills.

Second, because our electricity or car payment doesn't depend on "getting out even," getting lucky, making money on the next trade, or making money on most of our trades, we are far more likely to trade correctly by doing the right things, mainly by honoring our stops and cutting losses as quickly as possible.

Third, doing other things and having other interests and will get our mind off the markets and that is a good thing. Trading is a mentally and physically demanding activity because we must constantly fight and control our emotions. Traders need regular breaks.

Diversify mentally

Ironically, not caring so much and thus trading with detachment is likely to make us better traders. Experienced and skilled traders know that even a string of losses results in only a small drawdown of their capital if they strictly limit their risk. Thus, they do not worry about every dollar and do not obsess over getting out of a bad trade only after breaking even. They quickly cut their losses and move onto better opportunities. They remain calm through winning and losing streaks. They are not too excited about profits nor anguished by losses. They focus on trading well and cutting losses on the next 1000 trades and beyond. This virtuous cycle is every trader's goal.

In short, not caring so much about the outcome of any individual trade is the second crucial foundation that complements risk management in the trader's toolkit.

By all means traders should put much effort into studying the markets and controlling their emotions. We must exercise strict discipline to trade only compelling set-ups. But after all the preparation, study, and deliberation, **we have to let go**. We have to say to ourselves and believe, "I am bigger than this trade. My life is much more than how this trade turns out or even whether I succeed as a trader." This exercise is not just a mental trick to make us better traders. It is the truth. Do we want our lives to be defined by a series of trades, no matter how profitable? Or even a lifetime of successful trading? Do we really think we are a failure if we don't succeed as a trader? It would indeed be a low bar to define our life based on a series of trades or whether we make it as a trader. We have a much better chance of succeeding as traders if we don't make it our sole occupation, passion, and interest.

I often think a 5th grader could be a formidable classical chartist likely to outperform most adult traders. The kid hunts for well-formed chart patterns and picks one. After entering a trade, the mentor tells the kid: okay, go out and play. Explore the playground. Ride your bike. Just go have fun and forget about this trade. Eat five scoops of ice cream. Play catch or tag. Linger in the yard as the sun sets. We'll come back in a couple weeks and see what happened. If the trade was profitable, so be it. If the trade failed, then we'll move on to the next compelling chart pattern. This would be an excellent trading routine.

Yes, we should devote serious effort to studying classical charting but we must also live our life. The truth is that the best books on classical charting are not difficult. The principles and suggestions are logical and straightforward. The great difficulty is remembering and following the rules because our emotions will constantly push us to bad trading practices. We will find it necessary to constantly review and remind ourselves of good trading practices because we tend to forget so easily and we are so very stubborn. We are our own worst enemy.

So I am suggesting that we be open to the possibility that we may not be successful over the long run as a chart trader. I believe this acknowledgement increases my chances of being a successful trader over the long run. By trading with just a portion of my savings, pursuing other opportunities and interests, and continuously acquiring diverse skills and knowledge, I am not so emotionally caught up on the success of my trading. And this detachment is crucial to trade well.

Some readers might ask if such acknowledgement of our limitations sets us up for failure. There is a chance that we will not commit seriously to studying the markets and trading well if we have other plans. Wouldn't it be better to say there is no turning back once we start trading? I don't think so. Optimism is good, but it must be balanced with planning and prudence, especially in trading. All of us will fail at many things in life, and some of us may not become successful traders. Failure in trading doesn't make us a bad person, nor should it mean losing our savings. But I believe a "do-or-die" attitude in trading makes a large financial loss much more likely. We should be mature enough to tackle a new challenge like trading without confusing the necessary dedication and patience with a destructive "my self-respect depends on making a fortune in trading" attitude. **Mix energy and dedication with intellectual modesty, maturity, and perspective.** Adopting this outlook is not preparing for failure but wisely acknowledging that we cannot know everything and that it is smart to prepare for contingencies.

Benjamin Graham's doubts about fundamental investing

Let me make one more appeal for intellectual modesty in all our endeavors. Consider what Benjamin Graham, a great investor and Warren Buffett's teacher, said about his profession (picking individual stocks with the goal of beating the broader market) in his book *The Intelligent Investor*:

> [W]e must consider the possibilities ... of making *individual* [stock] selections which are likely to prove more profitable than an across the board average. What are the prospects of doing this successfully? We would be less than frank ... if we did not at the outset express **some grave reservations** on this score. ... [T]here is considerable and impressive evidence ... that this is very hard to do, even though the qualifications of those trying it are of the highest. (emphasis added)

If the founder of value investing acknowledges the stiff and perhaps insurmountable challenges of stock picking, then perhaps classical chartists should also consider the limitations of charting. Graham did not say that it was impossible to beat the market although I think he came very close to saying so. He said it was very difficult to beat the market and that intelligent investors must not take unintelligent risks while trying. "Margin of safety" was one of Graham's contributions to investing. By investing in stocks with a built-in margin of safety, and it is not easy to find such stocks, investors reduced the risk of losing money but were not guaranteed of beating the market. Similarly, traders can increase their odds of, but never guarantee, long-term success by minimizing their losses and only making bets on chart patterns with a highly favorable reward-to-risk possibility.

The point of quoting Graham is not to say that Graham urged stock pickers to abandon fundamental stock analysis and become classical chartists. He did not. My point is that intellectual modesty is important. Realize that we are wrong often and that we do not have all the answers. It is wise and prudent to not stake all of our savings on one investment or trading approach.

Benjamin Graham on chart trading

Genius is eternal patience.

Michelangelo

So few succeed in the market because they want to get rich quickly.

Jesse Livermore

What Graham did say about technical analysis and charting in *Security Analysis*, his foundational book on fundamental investing, is very interesting and informative:

> Undoubtedly, **there are times** when the behavior of the market, as revealed on the charts, carried a definite and trustworthy meaning of particular value to those who are skilled in its interpretation. If reliance on chart indications were confined to those really convincing cases, a more positive argument could be made in favor of 'technical study.' But such **precise signals seem to occur only at wide intervals**, and in the meantime **human impatience** plus the exigencies of the chart reader's profession **impel him to draw more frequent conclusions from less convincing data.** (emphasis added)

The point is not that Graham embraced charting although it is very interesting that Graham, the father of fundamental analysis, said that charting can be useful. Graham's critique points to one of the most important ingredients for success in trading, investing, and many things in life: patience.

As traders, we will periodically lose focus and discipline and make suboptimal bets. We were too impatient to wait for the charts to tell a clear picture. Then we are eager to make up the losses by making more bets on unfavorable set-ups. We are afraid that if we don't trade these suboptimal patterns then the market will not offer any more trading opportunities. We lose more money and the destructive cycle continues. And we are too exhausted mentally and financially to take advantage of the inevitable reappearance of favorable set-ups.

If there is only one thing we get out of this book, that one thing should be the confident knowledge that there will always, always, and always be new trading opportunities. Be patient. The market is not going anywhere. Patience gives us the ultimate freedom to place bets only on favorable trade set-ups. **It is accurate to describe the trader's routine as not one of constantly trading but mostly waiting, observing, and waiting some more and only intermittently entering trades**. Incidentally, when on a losing streak, closing all positions and walking away from the screen for a couple of days or even weeks can be very helpful. The market, and new opportunities, will always be there.

Let's conclude. The most important way I recognize my limitations – that I may be momentarily lucky, that classical charting may be a trading approach with deep flaws that I don't know about, or that even if classical charting is an effective trading method I may not be good enough to consistently profit from it over the long run – is that I diversify my savings. Regardless of market conditions, I only trade with a portion of my savings.

Knowing that I have a financial cushion gives me the confidence to take calculated risks. And informed speculating is none other than taking risks that offer a potentially large gain at the risk of a relatively small loss.

Wrap up

Experienced traders may skip Chapter 3 where I discuss the most basic tools of trading.

I wrote Chapter 3 because I wanted everyone, including people who have never looked at a stock chart, to feel comfortable learning about trading stocks using chart patterns. While my goal was not to write an encyclopedia on trading, my goal was to give the novice trader as inviting a learning environment as possible.

My goal is not to make all of us classical chartists. My goal is to do my best to help us decide whether we might consider trading stocks using classical charting. If we decide after reading this book that trading is not for us, then we should be proud of having made the effort to explore a new idea.

CHAPTER 4
Basic Trading Tools

Simplicity is the ultimate form of sophistication.

Leonardo da Vinci

Bar chart

Let's start from the beginning. What is a price chart? The following chart of Cray Inc. (the supercomputer maker) is an example of a stock's price chart.

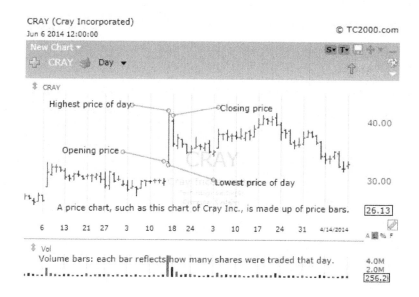

This price chart records the price history of Cray using price bars. A price chart that uses price bars is also called a bar chart. While there are other ways to visualize a stock's price history, I prefer price bars and bar charts.

Let's examine the components of the price bar. Look at the long price bar in Cray's price chart. The top of every bar tells us the highest price at which the stock traded that day and the bottom of the bar tells us the lowest traded price of the day. The short horizontal hypen-like line sticking out on the left of the price bar tells us the price at which the stock opened for trading that day. And the short line sticking out on the right side of the price bar tells us the closing price for the day.

Timeframes

I use daily, weekly, and monthly price charts in my trading. I use weekly and monthly charts to get a big-picture view of a stock's price history while I use daily charts to make entry and exit decisions. On weekly and monthly charts, each price bar represents a week's and month's worth of trading, respectively.

I almost never look at timeframes shorter than a day. I don't look at 1-minute or 15-minute charts. I occasionally look at 1-hour charts.

I do not intentionally day trade although sometimes a position I entered in the morning may be stopped out by the end of the day and this same-day round-trip is a day trade.

Charting programs

Let's talk about online charting programs. Charting programs display continuously updated price charts of stocks and other financial instruments. I use TC2000's charting service because I have found it easy to use with good customer support. You may choose to use another charting package as there are several good ones available. Be sure to try different services and choose the one that you feel most comfortable with. I like simplicity, and I have found TC2000 allows me to keep things as simple as possible. On the right side of my main monitor is my list of stocks that I scroll through while the rest of the screen displays the price chart. I use a horizontal strip at the bottom of my screen to view volume bars. That's it. I also have convenient tab buttons that I can click to switch between daily, weekly, and monthly charts.

Again, experiment and choose a charting service that makes things easy for you.

Understand that classical charting does not require us to install 20 screens showing dozens of indicators. Successful chart trading does not require fancy chart programs and expensive equipment.

The most important battle will not be on the screen but in our minds.

Online brokers

I use two discount online brokers. I have my trading capital split into two accounts as a form of diversification. Not having all of my funds in one location acts as a brake during bouts of greed and fear and helps prevent rash decisions. There are several good discount online brokers. As with charting programs, we should try several of them and then choose. We may simply choose the broker with the lowest commissions. That is perfectly fine. We do not need fancy brokers with high commissions to trade well.

Online brokers are in a fierce competition to earn our business. After we have traded with a brokerage for a while, we can call customer service and ask for a discount on the commission rate. Even if a brokerage advertises its commission as, say, $9 a trade, it will be open to offering us a lower commission to keep our business. One of my brokers reduced my commission by 30%.

Our charting program and broker should always play a mere secondary role in our trading. No amount of high-end customer service or the most sophisticated charting features will guarantee profits. How well we control our emotions and apply good trading practices will determine our long-term success. Keep it simple and be patient.

<u>We're ready</u>

Now we know how to read the price chart of a stock that is displayed on our charting program. And we are ready to spot patterns on a stock chart. At first we may see patterns where none exist. We will force meaning onto a chart for the sake of finding a pattern. We might even think that all good patterns are gone and that we will have to force it to make money. We will always be wrong if we think that good patterns will stop forming. We need to be patient.

Spotting classical chart patterns does not guarantee profits. Just because we find a textbook chart pattern doesn't guarantee that we will successfully manage our emotions to properly enter and manage the trade. Also, the "perfect" chart pattern may fail to break out or fail after breaking out and transform into something entirely different. The only thing we can do is to enter compelling set-ups with advantageous reward-to-risk possibilities and, as we discussed in Chapter 3, let go.

Let's begin.

PART II

CLASSICAL CHART PATTERNS

CHAPTER 5
Head & Shoulders Top

The first classical pattern we'll look at is the Head & Shoulders top pattern. A H&S top can form after a significant uptrend and indicates a possible trend reversal that leads to a price decline.

<u>Boeing: 2-year H&S top</u>

The following weekly chart, where each price bar represents a week's price range, shows a massive textbook H&S top that formed in Boeing from May 2006 to June 2008 with a decisive breakdown that penetrated the neckline in late June 2008:

FIGURE 1

A valid H&S top pattern must have 3 peaks with the middle peak, the head, rising above the shoulder peaks and the two shoulders must have some overlap in price, and the more overlap the better. The pattern should form after a significant rise in price. That is, a reversal pattern must have something to reverse. A H&S top's neckline connects the bottom of the left shoulder to the bottom of the head. A H&S top is completed when prices decisively close below the neckline after forming the right shoulder.

Beyond these essential features, there are many variations to the H&S top. As we gain experience looking at charts, we will learn to focus our attention on well-formed patterns and ignore the rest.

Every chart offers important lessons. Some of the takeaways from Boeing's H&S top are:

First, we, especially beginners, should strive to trade only chart patterns that are as well formed as this H&S top. Of course just because a pattern is textbook-perfect doesn't mean the pattern will work and be profitable. In fact, even "perfect"-looking patterns will fail most of the time. The point is that we should not force meaning onto charts where there is none. We must not project our hopes, dreams, and wishes onto charts. Classical chart patterns that are potential candidates for trading should be clearly defined and easy to spot. There was no doubt when looking at Figure 1 that Boeing was forming a possible H&S top pattern.

Second, a weekly chart is a valuable way to see the big picture. Though I make almost all entry and exit decisions based on a stock's daily chart, I always check the weekly chart to get a sense of the overall context in which a pattern is forming.

This massive H&S top in Boeing was so big that a trader would have likely missed this topping pattern if looking only at a daily chart. It would have been a case of losing sight of the forest for the trees. And while such big patterns are not very common, they are common enough to justify the regular review of weekly charts.

Third, and this point will be stressed many times, we must be patient. Many patterns take months and sometimes, like Boeing's H&S top, years to develop. While there are many shorter patterns ranging from days to several weeks discussed in this book, know that significant reversals of trend take time to develop. Also note how prices entered a narrow trading range for three months after breaking down through the neckline. Three months is a long time to be staring at our screen everyday waiting for the big move down. The smart trader would enter the trade, set a stop, and go do other things. Of course Boeing's stock could have moved up and triggered our stop-loss order. If so, so be it. We incurred a small loss and would move on to other set-ups.

Apple: 5-week H&S top

Our next H&S top is a 5-week pattern that formed in Apple from September to October of 2012. This H&S top was small in size but not in effect as it started a 40% price decline in Apple shares:

<u>FIGURE 2</u>

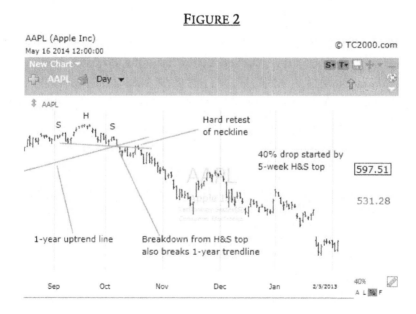

What can we learn from this pattern?

First, every principle has exceptions. While major reversal patterns can take months or years to develop, they can also form quickly as it did in

Apple. Thus, we must never place a bet without regard to risk relying on a rule that is "supposed to work." There is no such thing. Price is the ultimate rule.

Second, we should never ignore H&S patterns, including small ones. H&S patterns are one of the most reliable classical patterns. They are also one of the most versatile patterns because if a H&S top doesn't work, a "H&S top failure" is a distinct pattern that can offer compelling trading opportunities. We'll cover H&S failure patterns in Chapter 16.

Third, notice that prices broke down through the neckline of the H&S top and the 1-year trendline at the same time. Such interesting coincidences are common in classical charting. The fact that these two developments coincided did not guarantee that the pattern would work. But, at least in my mind, these twin developments increased the likelihood of a powerful trend reversal.

Fourth, note the hard retest of the neckline. **Retests are price reversals after breakout that re-challenge the breakout boundary.** Here, after breaking down through the neckline of the H&S top, prices reversed and closed slightly above the neckline before breaking down in a sustained downtrend. Some retests lead to pattern failure while others stop at or short of the breakout boundary. All retests challenge our poise. We cannot know if or when retests will occur. We must be ready for them.

After we view some more charts to get a feel for classical chart patterns, we will discuss in depth how we can enter trades and set stop-loss orders. There is no rule that works ideally every time. For now, know that retests of key pattern boundaries happen often and that the only thing we can control is our entry and stop points.

Lastly, let's discuss short sales of stocks. Shorting allows a trader to profit from price declines in stocks. Since there are both bullish (pointing to a possible increase in price) and bearish (pointing to a possible decline in price) classical chart patterns, buying and shorting stocks allows us to use the full range of classical charting tools.

That said, I understand some of us may be apprehensive about shorting a stock, especially if we have never done so. I was unfamiliar with the concept of shorting when I started to trade. Some of us may have ethical objections to shorting. We don't have to short stocks, but we should make our decision after learning about shorting, and, if we are open to it, trying some very small short sales to gain familiarity. We should decide based on knowledge rather than fear. And if we decide to add shorting to our trading kit, we can always trade a smaller size when shorting as I usually do.

ICA: 11-week H&S top

As noted, there are many variations to each classical pattern. The following H&S top in ICA, a Mexican construction company, shows one of my favorite variations in a H&S top:

FIGURE 3

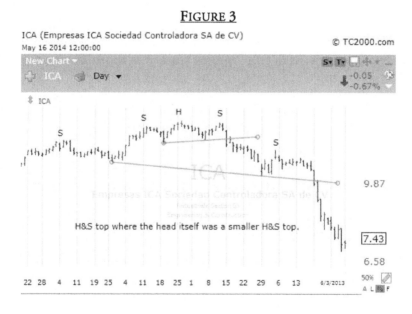

First, note the head of this 4-month H&S top was itself a smaller H&S top pattern. I find this pattern-within-a-pattern very interesting just as a visual phenomenon. It can also have great practical value as it can offer us the opportunity to enter a trade earlier than otherwise. For example, here, we might consider shorting shares upon the completion of the smaller H&S top pattern, then perhaps shorting additional shares upon completion of the larger H&S top. Every situation will be different, and just because we have a pattern-within-a-pattern does not mean we will have an early, or any, entry opportunity. And we must remember that even the most promising textbook patterns fail, and fail often.

Second, note the down-sloping neckline. Necklines and key boundaries need not be perfectly horizontal. They can be up-sloping or down-sloping. I prefer to trade patterns with boundaries that are as horizontal as possible because they clearly indicate the major highs and lows that must be overcome for a decisive breakout. We will talk more about the merits of horizontal vs. slanting pattern boundaries in later chapters.

Third, despite there being many legitimate and compelling variations to the textbook H&S pattern, we should try, especially as beginners, to stick as much as possible to trading patterns that resemble the textbook form. Too often traders label a chart as a H&S top even though none of the basic requirements of the pattern are met. Traders who appear in the media are not immune from making this error. I think it is beneficial to follow the principles spelled out by Schabacker and Edwards & Magee, especially regarding pattern shape. I do not follow everything that the founders of classical charting say in their books, but I do follow their physical requirements for the classical patterns.

LifeLock, Inc.: 2-month H&S top

The next H&S top is a chance to apply what we learned from Apple's H&S top. We see LifeLock breaking down from a H&S top, and this breakdown coincided with the breaking of a yearlong uptrend line:

FIGURE 4

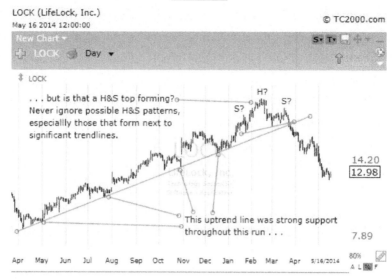

The next chart zooms in on the H&S top and breakout area:

FIGURE 4.1

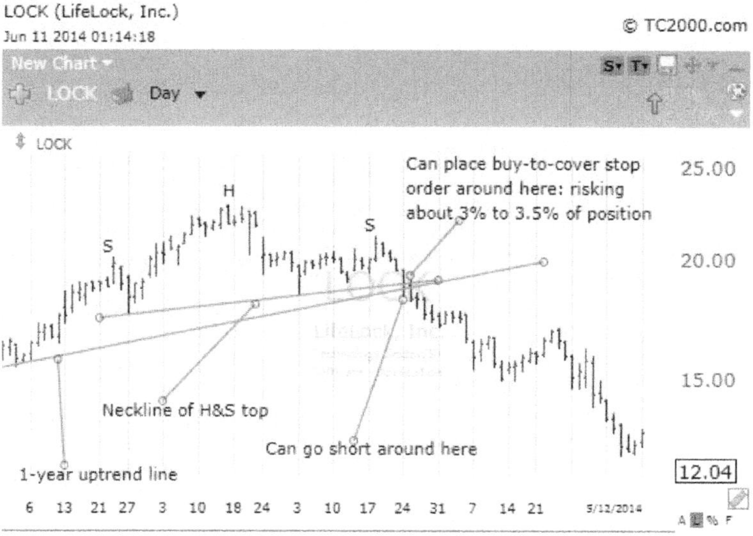

Let's talk about how much we might risk on a trade. It seems most professional traders risk no more than 1% of their trading account on a single trade. I think most traders and especially beginners should not risk more than 0.4% to 0.8% of their account on a trade. While our risk tolerance and trading capital will vary, we must pursue risk management and the limitation of losses as our most important goals. For example, if our trading account is $50,000, we should risk no more than $200 (0.4% of $50,000) to $400 (0.8% of $50,000) on any individual trade. These are general guidelines and I think the more cautious we are, the better.

Let's use the next chart that shows a H&S top that formed in QQQ, the ETF that tracks the Nasdaq 100 index, to see what these risk guidelines mean in terms of the nuts and bolts of entering and exiting a trade.

Classical patterns form in the major stock indexes and the ETFs that track them just as in individual stocks. I always watch closely the index ETFs – SPY for S&P 500, QQQ for Nasdaq 100, DIA for Dow Jones Industrial Average, and IWM for the Russell 2000 index – to get a sense of the overall market. While I trade mostly individual stocks, I also know that most stocks move with the overall market. So if the market indexes are dropping sharply, then I will be more cautious about trading bullish set-ups.

QQQ: 6-week H&S top

The following chart shows a H&S top that formed in QQQ, the ETF that tracks the Nasdaq 100 index, from August to October 2012:

FIGURE 5

QQQ (PowerShares QQQTrust Ser 1)
Jun 12 2014 12:01:10
© TC2000.com

New Chart ▾   S▾ T▾
QQQ ≡ Day ▾   -0.39
-0.42%

$ QQQ

Closing price the day before breakout: 68.35   72.00
H   Breakout day (i.e., last
S   day) high: 68.18   70.00
S   Retest high: 68.30
68.00

66.00

Breakout day closing price: 67.26   64.00

62.00

6   13   20   27   4   10   17   24   1   8   15   22   31   5   11/20/2012

If we have a $30,000 trading account and we don't want to risk more than 0.7% of our account on any single trade, then we have $210 (0.7% of $30,000) to risk on this H&S top. Let's say that we decide to short shares at the breakout day's closing price of 67.26. Where might we place our buy-to-cover stop order that will cut our losses should the breakout reverse and the pattern fail? I use the **last day rule**, a concept I learned from Peter L. Brandt, to place most of my stops. How does it work? For short trades, we place our stop just above the high of the last day in which prices traded above the breakout boundary. For long trades, we place our stop just below the low of the last day in which prices traded below the breakout boundary.

Here, following the last day rule would mean placing a stop just above 68.18, say, at 68.20 or so. Some of us may prefer to give more cushion to our stops. If we do, then we must keep our potential loss within our maximum risk tolerance. Note that a buy-to-cover stop order at 68.20 is very close to and barely above the neckline of the H&S top. A stop at 68.20 seems at risk of getting triggered by mere normal price volatility in QQQ. Indeed, QQQ experienced a hard retest after breaking down through the neckline. While prices did not close above the neckline, they did trade above it by trading as high as 68.30. Placing a stop at 68.20 or even 68.25 meant we got stopped out.

By the way, there is absolutely nothing wrong with getting stopped out. Remember, classical chartists can have more losing trades than winning trades and still be profitable overall. Risk management, not profits, is our priority. So getting stopped out for a very modest loss means we are managing risk.

As we noted, every rule has exceptions. While I faithfully apply the last day rule in most of my trades, the particularities of this H&S top meant we had to consider placing our place a stop a bit farther away from the neckline to account for normal price volatility, including a possible retest. So we modify the last day rule. Here, I would look at the price range on the day before the breakout. The closing price on the day before the breakout was 68.35. Placing a stop just above this closing price, say, at about 68.37 or 68.40, is a reasonable choice. If we want even more leeway, then we may choose to place a stop just above the high of the day before the breakout. Remember that the more leeway we give a trade, the more likely we have to use a smaller position to keep our possible loss under our maximum-risk limit.

Every chart presents different entry and exit scenarios. Still, I have found in my trading that the last day rule usually works very well by placing my stop at a reasonable distance from the breakout boundary and from normal volatility and from even the reach of hard retests. When the last day rule does not produce a satisfactory stop point, I improvise. How I improvise is far less important than that I keep my possible maximum loss within my risk tolerance. Sometimes we'll just have to pick a spot. Nothing can protect us from prices just barely triggering our stop and then reversing and making a powerful run. We must not let such events frustrate us too much. Such hit and runs will happen to everyone no matter what rule we use to place our stops. There is nothing magical about the last day rule. It is simply a trading tool to manage risk. Some trades work out and others will not. We must accept this reality. Such ever-present uncertainty is the price we pay to limit our losses and stay in the game long enough until we gain enough experience to take advantage of great market conditions. Remember, there will always be other trades.

Let's go back to the QQQ set-up. Let's say we decide to place our stop at 68.37, just above the closing price of the day before breakout. We shorted shares at 67.26 and placed our stop at 68.37. That means we are risking $1.11 for every share of QQQ that we short. If we have a $30,000 account and we want to risk no more than 0.7% on any single trade, then we have $210 to risk for this trade. Divide $210 by $1.11, the distance in dollars from 67.26 to 68.37, and we get 189.1. So we can short 189 shares and likely limit our potential loss to $210 at our chosen entry (where we shorted) and exit (where we may buy to cover) spots. I always like to stay under my maximum risk, so I would short only about 180 shares. Of course, we may choose to further reduce our position size. A 180-share short position is the maximum size given our risk parameters.

There are several more points to discuss.

First, trading commissions will be another cost. If our broker charges us, say, $8 per trade, that means our round trip trading cost will be $16. Commissions add up. They are another reason why we should trade only compelling set-ups.

Second, we may lose more than we had planned if a stock **gaps up or down**. A gap up happens if, after we shorted 180 shares of QQQ at the closing price of 67.26 and placed a buy-to-cover stop at 68.37, the next day QQQ starts to trade at, say, 69.50. This overnight price jump up that produced a gap between today's and yesterday's price bars is called a gap up. An overnight jump down in price is a gap down. The result is that instead of losing only $1.11 a share, we would be stopped out with a loss of $2.24 for every share we shorted for a total loss of $403.20 plus trading commission. We lost almost twice as much as we were willing to risk on this trade. This scenario doesn't happen often but it is common enough that we must always be mindful of it and is one more reason why we must always diversify our trades and never bet our entire stake on one or even a series of trades. It is perfectly acceptable and expected to lose more than we had planned on some of our trades. What is important is that such greater-than-expected losses, which are unavoidable at times for everyone, mean nothing more than minor additional losses.

Third, we might have noticed that I did not include the volume bars for the charts we have analyzed so far. I have included volume bars in later charts where I thought volume was one of the decisive factors in making a trading decision. But I personally have found that volume is often not a decisive factor in many of my trades. Edwards & Magee stress the importance of volume. And volume is often a vital clue, especially in situations when the volume conforms to the textbook descriptions laid out by Edwards & Magee. But I have found that textbook classical patterns form and work a lot of times without volume confirmation. So, volume, while important, is only one factor in my decision-making and the lack of volume confirmation doesn't disqualify a pattern to me. In short, volume is like any other factor in trading and classical charting: it is not a guarantee that "must" and "should" work. Prices will do whatever they want to do. Risk management is the only thing we can control.

However, volume is always a crucial factor in thinly-traded or low-volume stocks. Thin stocks tend to be more volatile and more risky. I often pass on a promising pattern developing in a low-volume stock because the extreme volatility makes entering and exiting a trade within my risk parameters so difficult. The lure of thin stocks is that powerful moves happen quickly and thus we may make a lot of money quickly. But I have found that it is much easier to lose a lot of money quickly with thin stocks. So I usually stay away from them.

Fourth, where might we take profits if the trade is successful? So far, we have concentrated, properly, on placing our stop orders so that we limit our losses if the trade fails. While risk management is our first goal, we trade to make money, and taking profits is an important skill. Classical charting provides a general guideline for taking profits in the form of the size of the pattern that launches the up or down move. The height of a classical pattern's widest point is used to project or "measure" the possible up or down move from the breakout point. So, in the H&S top pattern in QQQ, we measure the distance from the top of the head to the neckline and project that distance down from the breakout point. This measurement is the minimum move that could happen.

But, again, as with all "rules" in classical charting, these profit-projections are general guidelines. As I have repeated and will repeat many more times, the only thing traders can control is risk management. Patterns, even after decisive breakouts, fail often. When prices, after a decisive breakdown from a textbook H&S top pattern, reverse and go straight up, we must take our small loss according to our pre-determined stop-loss level and get out of the trade. We must not stay in the trade and refuse to take our now rapidly-growing losses because "the measurement rule guarantees that prices will soon go in the right direction (down) again and produce the projected profit." Wrong. The only guarantee in the financial markets is that risk, indeed catastrophic risk, is everywhere. Traders work with this harsh reality, but traders can do so on their terms by always diversifying their trades, always honoring their pre-determined stops, and getting out with a small loss if the trade doesn't work out.

We said that the general rule is that the projected move is the minimum move that could happen. Look again at the small H&S top that produced a massive 40% decline in the price of Apple shares. The takeaways from Apple's H&S top are that we should never ignore a H&S top pattern whatever its size and that there is no correct answer as to when to take profits. There was no way to know that this small H&S top would lead to a 40% decline. If we took profits after a 20% decline and happily looked elsewhere for other trade set-ups, then we should not be angry or embarrassed about the stock continuing to drop. Even here we must remember that there will always be more opportunities.

CHAPTER 6
Head & Shoulders Bottom

The head and shoulders bottom pattern is just that: a H&S top pattern turned upside down.

<u>Caesars Entertainment: 5-month H&S bottom</u>

Here is our first H&S bottom pattern:

FIGURE 6

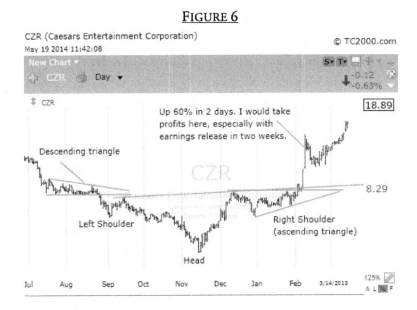

CZR (Caesars Entertainment Corporation)
May 19 2014 11:42:08
© TC2000.com

New Chart ▾
CZR   Day ▾   ↓-0.12   -0.63%

‡ CZR   18.89

Up 60% in 2 days. I would take profits here, especially with earnings release in two weeks.

Descending triangle

CZR

8.29

Left Shoulder

Right Shoulder (ascending triangle)

Head

Jul   Aug   Sep   Oct   Nov   Dec   Jan   Feb   3/14/2013   125%   A L ▦ F

The H&S bottom has three valleys with the middle valley, the head, deepest. Note how this H&S bottom's right shoulder took the form of an ascending triangle. We will discuss ascending triangles in Chapter 9. So we have another pattern-within-a-pattern and a decisive breakout from the ascending triangle coincided with the breakout from the H&S bottom. As we will see here and in other charts, **the more powerful the breakout, the more difficult it can be, and sometimes too risky, to enter the trade.** The next chart focuses on the breakout from the right shoulder:

FIGURE 6.1

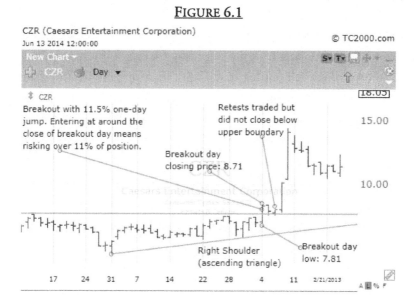

Caesars Entertainment's stock jumped 11.5% on the breakout day. Buying shares at around the closing price of the breakout day and placing our stop just below the low meant risking over 11% of our position. That is a lot to risk and I would avoid trading such a set-up unless the pattern was very promising and the breakout decisive. As this H&S bottom had good form and produced a decisive breakout, I would look to trade this breakout if I can buy a reasonably-sized position while staying within my risk limit.

If our trading account is $50,000 and we don't want to risk more than 1% of our account on any single trade, that means we have $500 to risk on this trade. Entering at 8.71 and placing a stop at 7.80 means risking $0.91 on every share of CZR stock we buy. We divide $500 by $0.91 and get 549. So, we can buy around 540 shares for $4703 and stay under our maximum risk barring any gap downs in price. (I usually round down to account for commissions and to get an even number.) I think this entry and stop-loss placement constitutes a prudent and promising trade given the pattern and breakout.

There are alternative entry and exit strategies.

One option is to buy a larger position at the closing price of 8.71. Assuming the same $50,000 account, how do we risk no more than 1% of our account on this trade? We move our stop up and place it closer to the horizontal upper boundary of the ascending triangle. If we raise our stop to, say, $8.08, rather than putting it at $7.80, then we can buy 790 shares for $6880 and stay within our $500 maximum risk. I did not use a magic formula to pick 8.08 as an alternative stop placement. I picked 8.08 because it seemed reasonably far below the upper boundary of the ascending triangle to not get triggered too easily by normal volatility. That said, a hard retest or even just normal volatility has a much higher chance of triggering a stop at 8.08 than at 7.80. If our higher stop survives, then we make more because we have a larger position. But if prices trigger our stop and then turn around and shoot up, then we lose $500 and miss a 60% surge in two days. We took a calculated risk and lost. But we traded the set-up well. We took a good swing at a compelling set-up while staying within our risk parameter. We suffered a minor loss and we move on to the next promising pattern. We cannot control prices. We can only control how we manage risk.

There is a second option. We can place a buy-stop order in anticipation of a breakout from the right shoulder. So far we have discussed stop orders in the context of **getting out** of a trade if the trade doesn't work. Stop orders can be also be used to **enter** trades. In the H&S tops discussed above, we could have placed a stop order to sell short a chosen number of shares at a level somewhere below the necklines. Such an order would be filled by our brokers if prices traded at that level.

For Caesars Entertainment's H&S bottom, we can place a stop order to buy a certain number of shares at a price somewhere above the upper boundary of the ascending triangle right shoulder:

FIGURE 6.2

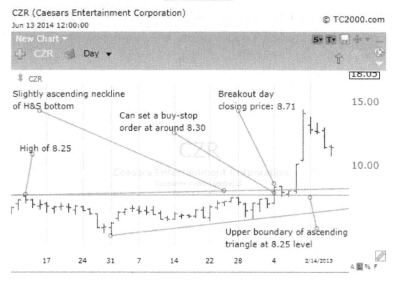

Let's say we choose to place a buy-stop order at 8.30, which is above the horizontal boundary of the right-shoulder ascending triangle and just below the slightly ascending neckline of the larger H&S bottom. If prices trigger our buy-stop order at 8.30 and continue to go up to break out of the H&S bottom, then we have the advantage of having entered earlier at a lower price. Entering earlier means that we can buy a larger position and still place our stop below the low of the breakout day. If we have a $50,000 account and faithfully follow the maximum 1% loss per trade rule, we have $500 to risk on this trade. Entering the trade at 8.30 and placing our stop at 7.80 means I can risk $0.50 per share. We divide $500 by $.50 and get 1000. We can buy 1000 shares, which is a 25% larger position than buying at 8.71 and using a higher stop, for $8300 plus commissions and yet give our position much more cushion to survive normal volatility and even hard retests. We also have the potential to earn significantly more profits should the trade work.

Important point: whenever I use a stop order to enter a trade, I always use it as part of a One Triggers Another (OTA) order. For example, the night before what may be the breakout day for Caesars Entertainment's

H&S bottom, I enter a stop order to buy 1000 shares at 8.30 that, when triggered, enters another order, a stop-loss order that will trigger if the breakout fails and prices decline to my pre-determined stop level. Every trade must have an exit order, a sell stop for a long position and a buy-to-cover stop for a short trade.

<u>Drawbacks to using stop orders to enter trades</u>

As with any trading tool, buy-stop and short-sell-stop orders do not always work well. Here are some of their drawbacks.

First, our buy-stop order could be triggered by a false breakout or an out-of-line price move. These are price moves that spend only part of the day outside the pattern boundary and then retreat back inside the boundary by the end of the trading day. These retreats can also trigger our stops. Again, there is nothing wrong with being stopped out for a small loss. As we know, we must be ready to take many small losses. But losses can add up, and more importantly, they can exhaust us mentally. **And preserving our mental capital is just as important as safeguarding our trading account**. Every trade is a calculated leap of faith. While we can keep risk at manageable levels by always diversifying our trades and following other prudent rules, we still need confidence to take swings at set-ups. **If we lose our nerve, then we cannot trade well**. Repeatedly getting stopped out by false breakouts will weaken our trading psyche. So when the real breakout happens, we feel too spent financially and psychologically to make an appropriate bet. We have lost our nerve. And the inability to take calculated risks can be just as frustrating as a string of losses.

Thus, there are advantages to waiting towards the end of the trading day to see if prices will close decisively above the pattern boundary and then manually entering a trade. The closing price is the most important price because it indicates where many traders felt comfortable holding their positions over night. My experience has been that most trades, including many of the best set-ups, gave me plenty of time to enter manually toward the end of the breakout day. Looking at the charts above, we did not have to use stop orders to short the H&S top patterns in Apple, LifeLock, and QQQ. We could have entered around the closing price towards the end of the breakout day.

Of course, there will be set-ups when not using a stop order to buy or short will mean missing the trade because it would be too late and too risky to enter after prices have broken out and travelled far away from the boundary. But that's trading. We catch some, and we miss some. If we miss a breakout from a pattern that we've been watching for weeks, months, or even years, we have to remember that there will always be more and better opportunities. So when, not if, we miss a trade, we must quickly move on.

The second potential drawback to entering a trade using a stop order is our old enemy: gap ups and gap downs. Actually, we can think of gap ups and downs as valuable friends because the ever-present possibility of price gaps forces us to never risk too much on any trade. As we will see, devastating price gaps of 40% and 50%, while rare, do occur. Such a huge loss on a position that represents 8% or 10% of our trading account will sting but overall is still a very manageable setback. But a 50% loss on a position that represents our entire account is far, far worse and something that we must avoid through prudent diversification and risk management.

Coming back to Caesars Entertainment, let's say that the stock price had opened at 9.50 on the breakout day after an overnight gap up and then immediately reversed and dropped straight down back into the pattern and triggered our stop. (In real life the stock opened at 7.85 and closed at 8.71 on the breakout day.) If we had a buy-stop order for 1000 shares at 8.30, then we would find that this buy-stop order, which is a market order that triggers at the current trade price, was filled once prices were at or above 8.30. Since the stock, after the overnight gap up, started to trade at 9.50, our buy-stop order was filled at 9.50. We paid $1.20 more than we had planned for each of our 1000 shares. And when our stop was triggered at 7.80, our losses were $1.70 per share compared to the $0.50 per share that we had allotted for this trade.

The result is that we lost $1,700 on this trade. If we have a $50,000 account, a $1,700 loss represents a 3.4% loss of capital. Such a loss stings, but it need not be anything more than that. Our trading account is still essentially intact and we simply move on.

We cannot predict overnight price gaps, but we can still mitigate their potential damage. One way is to only rarely use stop orders to buy or short. Another way is to use a smaller position size when using a stop order to potentially enter a trade. We can always add to our position if circumstances permit.

If we feel that a potential breakout from an explosive pattern seems "catchable" only through a stop order to buy or short but we prefer to enter a trade manually, then we can simply not trade. It takes much wisdom, patience, and strength to pass on a trade. It will be easier to pass on a trade if we remember that there will always be more opportunities.

A couple of other takeaways from this H&S bottom in Caesars Entertainment.

First, always look for patterns within larger patterns. The smaller pattern can give us an early entry point and also help us identify and make sense of the larger pattern.

Second, most patterns take time to develop. This H&S bottom took five months to form.

Third, breakouts can move very fast. So fast, in fact, that we may miss it or we may decide to not trade it. Our task is not to trade every breakout. Our task is doing the right thing, and that can mean not trading a breakout.

Callidus Software: 10-month H&S bottom

This H&S bottom's right shoulder was a rectangle pattern:

FIGURE 7

The next chart focuses on the breakout from the right shoulder:

FIGURE 7.1

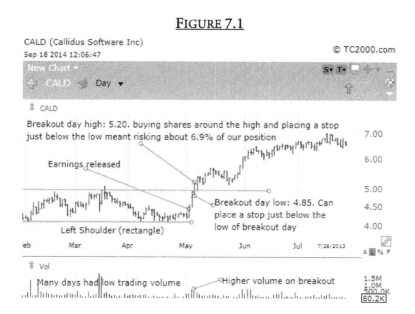

Let's again assume that we have a $50,000 trading account and we don't want to risk more than 1% ($500) of our total capital on any single trade.

Entering at the high (5.20) of the breakout day and placing our stop just below the low, say, at 4.84, means we risk $0.36 a share, which still allows us to buy almost 1390 shares ($500 divided $0.36) for about $7,200. Such an entry and exit gave us the possibility but never a guarantee to profit significantly from a continued breakout from a promising pattern while placing our stop reasonably far away from the upper boundary of the right-shoulder rectangle to survive retests and significant volatility.

If the breakout in Callidus Software reversed and we were stopped out, this losing trade cost us about $500 from our $7,220 position. That's a 6.9% loss on our position but a 1% loss of our trading account. Most traders, especially beginners, would be wise to keep our maximum possible loss on any individual trade under 1% of our total account. As noted, it seems most professional traders stay under the 1% figure. If I were starting out again, I would try to keep my loss on any single trade to under 0.5% of my account. We will lose the most money when we lack experience in the markets. We need time to learn, and we might as well lose less money when we are at our worst.

Quarterly earnings reports

All publicly-traded companies report their financial results every three months. We must watch for upcoming earnings reports. It is entirely unpredictable how investors and traders react to earnings reports. A "good" earnings report can be seen as bad if there wasn't enough good news. A "bad" earnings report can be seen as good if there was less bad news than expected. Moreover, stock prices can crash even after an objectively good earnings report for any or no reason. There is no way to predict the market's reaction to earnings releases. Thus, we should not enter a position just before an earnings release nor hold a position through an earnings report.

Even if it seems prices are about to break out of a promising pattern, I stand aside and wait if an earnings report is to be released soon. It can be frustrating to not trade a promising breakout because of an imminent earnings release. But we must stand aside because the utter unpredictability of the market's reaction to earnings means that we have no way to manage risk. Here, again, it helps to remember that there will always be other patterns to trade.

Here, the market reacted favorably to Callidus Software's earnings report. The stock jumped the day after earnings were released. It was not until the next day prices went up again and broke through the upper boundary of the rectangle right shoulder and decisively closed above it. The timing of the earnings release and the market's reaction to it were favorable. The market's reaction was not so positive as to cause an explosive breakout that made entering the trade too risky. Prices increased strongly but still in a controlled pace that gave traders plenty of time to buy shares at prices that offered a favorable reward-to-risk possibility. Also, we could have more confidence in the breakout because the uncertainty surrounding the earnings release was out of the way. Note also that the volume on the breakout day was heavier than in previous days. Such volume confirmation makes it more likely, but never guarantees, that the breakout is significant.

There are no guarantees in trading except that we will lose a lot of money if we do not respect risk. One factor that increased the risk on this trade was that Callidus Software is a relatively low-volume stock. **I consider stocks whose daily volume is often under 100,000 shares to be thinly traded**. And I usually avoid stocks whose daily volume is often under 50,000 shares as they can be even more volatile. We can refer to a stock's Beta to get a sense of the stock's volatility but I rely mostly on what I see on the chart: CALD shares often had wide daily trading ranges. For example, the stock jumped 7.6%, 8.8%, 5.5%, and 3.9% in the days around the earnings report and breakout. Isn't that good for the trader who owns this stock? We must remember that what goes up quickly can come down even faster. There was no guarantee that the breakout from this H&S bottom would work even after prices closed decisively above the upper boundary of the right-shoulder rectangle. The market could have changed its initial positive reaction to the earnings report and pushed down prices anytime after breakout. And relatively low-volume stocks can crash very quickly.

Given this risk in low-volume stocks like CALD, a fine idea is to trade a smaller size here. We don't have to risk our maximum on every trade. Maybe we decide to risk only 0.5% or even less. Or perhaps we decide to skip this trade. That is perfectly acceptable as well. We always have a choice. Nobody forces us to trade. We need to evaluate every breakout with one overriding question in mind: do we have a favorable entry spot that limits risk?

As we've repeated many times already and as we will and must hear many more times: our number one task as traders is to manage risk and not to make money. Put another way: concentrate on doing the right thing rather than making money. When we manage risk in a systematic way, we will be able to trade for the long run.

The financial markets are always unpredictable, and quarterly earnings reports add another layer of risk and volatility. We can avoid the market's unpredictable reaction to earnings reports by simply not trading through earning releases. And risk and unpredictability are compounded in low-volume stocks.

Hewlett-Packard: 10-week H&S bottom

The next chart shows quarterly earnings reports producing very volatile price moves in Hewlett-Packard shares:

FIGURE 8

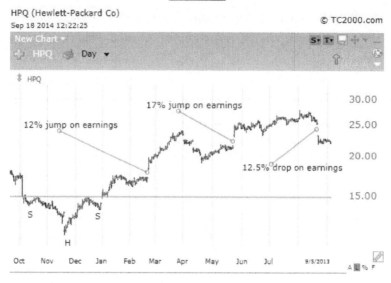

I know what many of us are thinking because I had the same thought: those 12% and 17% one-day price jumps seem too good to pass up so I'll just hold my position through earnings releases and hope that the market reacts positively to the earnings news. But these price increases could just as easily have been comparable or worse price drops. Indeed, Hewlett-Packard's stock declined by more than 12% on the third earnings report shown on the chart.

Recall our discussion about the distinction between informed trading and outright gambling. Informed trading is about entering at a spot on the chart that maximizes potential gains while defining and limiting risk. Yes, we expect to have more losing trades than winning trades. Yes, price gaps, up or down, unrelated to earnings news mean sometimes we lose more than we had planned. Yes, all financial activities involve risk. But we must not think that just because the financial markets are synonymous with uncertainty that there aren't degrees of risk. Trade entries and exits that are likely to keep losses within our risk parameters are not the same thing as taking a position before an earnings report on simply the hope of a positive markct reaction to the news. We have no way to quantify the market's future reaction to a report the contents of which we know nothing about.

That said, some of us (or is it all of us?) will, hopefully only occasionally, gamble on earnings reports. We should not do it, but some of us will give in to the temptation. If I were to hold a position through earnings reports, the following situation would be the only instance when I would consider doing so. The next chart focuses on the left portion of Figure 8 where the H&S bottom formed:

FIGURE 8.1

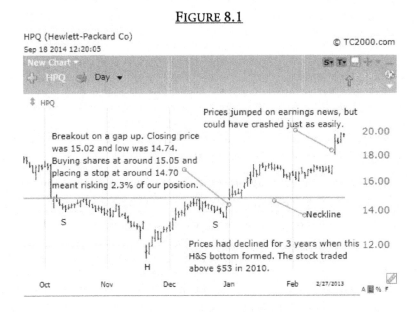

We have a H&S bottom and a breakout on a gap up in price. My experience has been that breakouts on price gaps tend to work more often than not. That said, we must never go all-in on any single pattern no matter how promising the breakout. Even textbook-perfect patterns fail often. Here, the gap-up in price was just another factor to consider when deciding whether to trade this pattern. I would trade this pattern given the symmetry of the H&S bottom (the left and right shoulders were about the same size), the breakout on a gap up, and a favorable entry spot. As noted on the chart, we risked about 2.3% of our position had we bought shares around the closing price of the breakout day and set our stop somewhere reasonably below the neckline.

If we had bought shares upon the breakout, we gained about 15% on our position in the next two weeks. Then prices traded in a narrow range for the next month and the quarterly earnings report was to be released soon. What now? The correct thing to do is to sell our entire position and book a 15% profit. But we are human, and we want more. If we are going to gamble, then we should do so with only a very small position. In this case, we would get lucky as the stock jumped 12% on the earnings report. Yes, we can do the wrong and irresponsible thing and get lucky and make money. But we will run out of luck and take a large hit to our trading capital if we continue to take such gambles. Doing the right thing means doing the unexciting thing over and over: honoring our stop, not chasing a missed breakout, not gambling, and just waiting. Doing the right thing doesn't guarantee profits, but it is the best way to be a long-term player in the trading game, and longevity is the best way to be profitable in the long run.

Lannett Co.: 5-month H&S bottom

Our next chart is another variation of the H&S bottom:

FIGURE 9

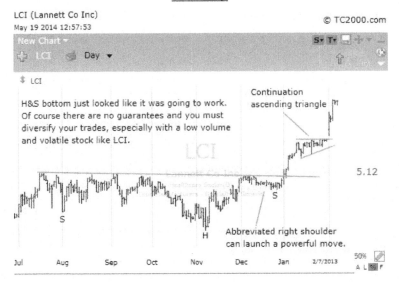

LCI (Lannett Co Inc)
May 19 2014 12:57:53
© TC2000.com

New Chart ▾   S▾ T▾
LCI   Day ▾

LCI

H&S bottom just looked like it was going to work.
Of course there are no guarantees and you must
diversify your trades, especially with a low volume
and volatile stock like LCI.

Continuation
ascending triangle

5.12

S

S

H

Abbreviated right shoulder
can launch a powerful move.

Jul   Aug   Sep   Oct   Nov   Dec   Jan   2/7/2013

Note that the right shoulder of the H&S bottom is much smaller than the left shoulder. While symmetry between the left and right shoulders is one of the defining traits of a textbook H&S pattern, as with all pattern "rules," there are exceptions. A H&S bottom such as this one where the right shoulder is significantly smaller than the left can launch a powerful move. It is as if the stock is itching to get moving and doesn't have the patience to form a right shoulder that is of similar size to the left shoulder.

Note also that this pattern gave us plenty of time to enter the trade. We could have bought shares toward the close of the breakout day or anytime during the next day. It was not necessary to use a buy-stop order to trade this breakout.

So was it as easy as buying shares once prices closed above the neckline of the H&S bottom? The major strike against this pattern was that the stock was very thinly-traded. Less than 20,000 shares traded per day on many days during pattern formation. As noted, I usually avoid stocks whose average daily volume is less than 50,000 shares. And I would recommend that beginners avoid entirely such low-volume stocks. As we gain experience, we may decide to trade, very carefully, some patterns that form in thin stocks. If I were to trade this H&S bottom pattern, I would use a position that was at most 30% to 40% of my normal position size.

Would I trade this set-up using a smaller position? Yes. The 6-month H&S bottom looked very promising with a clearly defined left shoulder and head. Another reason is that, despite the low volume, the stock traded relatively "cleanly," especially during the formation of the right shoulder. Thinly-traded stocks can jump wildly around and make risk control very difficult if not impossible. A stock's chart looks clean to me when there are few price gaps unrelated to pattern breakouts. As noted, breakouts on price gaps support but does not guarantee the validity of the breakout. The charts of some volatile stocks have price gaps almost every day. In contrast, Lannett's stock traded cleanly and in a tight range during the weeks leading up to the breakout.

Of course explosive volatility can appear anytime, especially in thin stocks, but the clean price action and low volatility during the formation of the right shoulder would be an important factor in support of not eliminating this pattern from my list of trade candidates. Yet it is perfectly acceptable to pass on this pattern because of the stock's low volume and the risk that accompanies a thin stock. Again, I recommend beginners to trade only stocks whose average daily volume is at least 200,000 shares.

Penn Virginia Corp.: 8-month H&S bottom

The next chart shows another pattern-within-a-pattern. Note how the breakout from the small symmetrical triangle launched the breakout from the larger H&S bottom:

FIGURE 10

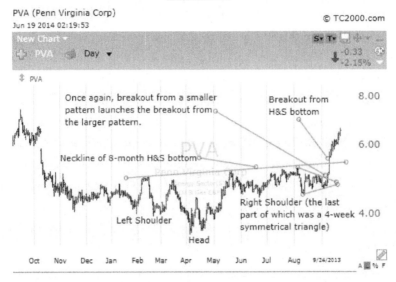

Now let's zoom in on the right shoulder area:

FIGURE 10.1

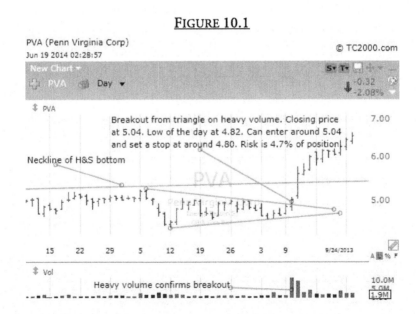

The breakout from the 4-week symmetrical triangle that constituted a portion of the right shoulder of this H&S bottom was an ideal spot to go long. This entire set-up – from the year-long H&S bottom pattern (the lengthier the build-up, the more powerful the breakout may be), the symmetrical-triangle right shoulder that offered an opportunity to enter early, and the textbook breakout on heavy volume – was very promising. Indeed, I would seriously consider risking more than my standard maximum risk and buy a larger position size. That said, I would still not risk more than 1.5% of my account even on such a promising pattern because there are no guarantees in trading. There are no rules that are supposed to work. This enticing H&S bottom that seems so promising? The market could care less as it can crash prices even after a decisive breakout. The pattern boundaries we draw are just that: nothing more than lines that we use as trading tools. The market and prices will do what they do. They are never wrong.

Always be cautious

By now we may have noticed a recurring theme. We discuss some exciting aspects of classical chart trading and then immediately remind ourselves of the utmost importance of caution. We may wish it were otherwise but catastrophic risk lurks everywhere in trading and the financial markets. If we are not careful, then we may lose it all. But we need not be pessimistic. We can learn to implement an uncompromising risk management strategy that allows us to be long-term players in the trading game. The only thing standing in the way of prudent risk management is ourselves.

Compelling set-ups such as this H&S bottom in Penn Virginia Corp. should motivate us to do the utmost to preserve our capital for the really promising charts. Such patterns can reaffirm our passion for trading. Of course we don't know which set-ups will work as even textbook patterns fail often. But one decisive winner can make up for many more small losses and produce overall profitability. If we lose our capital on suboptimal trades by chasing missed breakouts, entering at unfavorable spots, or just gambling outright, then we will be too exhausted financially and mentally to place a meaningful bet when a truly compelling pattern emerges.

I have experienced this painful situation many times. After losing money chasing breakouts and trading poorly formed patterns, I have simply lost the nerve to make a meaningful bet on the next promising trade. Then I watch from the sidelines as this pattern launches an explosive and very profitable trend. I get more frustrated. I chase this breakout by entering at a spot that carries more risk than my maximum-loss limit. I get stopped out and lose more money. I have lost not only my nerve, but also my detachment and my form. I am in a destructive cycle of negative feedback loops. When traders are in this situation, and all of us will be in this situation from time to time, we can exit our positions, walk away from the screen, and take a break from the market. We must rebuild our mental strength. We must regain our nerve, perspective, and balance. We must take our time. The market will always be there when we are ready to trade again.

Constantly reminding ourselves that there will always be more great set-ups can help us not chase missed breakouts and also give us the confidence to take a break. Even if we missed this Penn Virginia set-up, the existence of this and many other exciting patterns should remind us that we will always have the opportunity to make a comeback. The key is to be still standing when favorable market conditions reappear. And effective risk management keeps us in the arena.

United Community Banks: 7-month H&S bottom

Our next example shows yet another variation to the H&S bottom pattern. This time, the right shoulder took the form of a small H&S bottom:

FIGURE 11

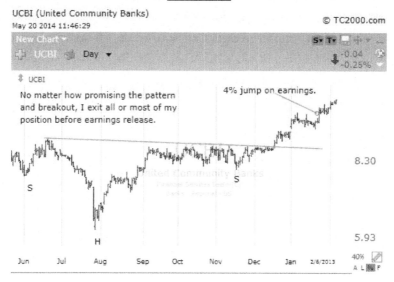

The next chart focuses on the right shoulder:

FIGURE 11.1

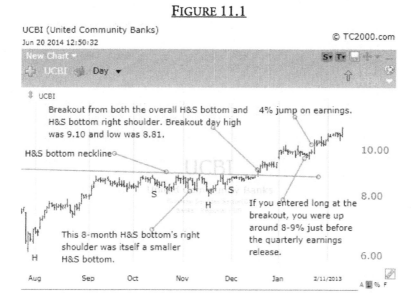

Here, we again have a situation where the next earnings report was to be released not so long after the breakout. If we bought shares around the closing price of the breakout day, we were up by about 8-9% on our position right before earnings release. What should we do? An almost 10% profit in less than a month is a good trade. I would sell my entire position, book my 10% profit, and move on to other set-ups. But the reality is that we are all susceptible to the temptation to gamble on earnings reports. And if we choose to gamble, and it's a choice as no one is forcing us to stay in this trade through the earnings report, I think we should gamble with no more than one-third of our original position.

CHAPTER 7
Continuation H&S Bottom

A continuation H&S bottom is a H&S bottom that forms after a sustained rise in prices and signals possibly another uptrend in prices.

<u>Deluxe Corp.: 2-month continuation H&S bottom</u>

Our first continuation H&S bottom pattern:

<u>FIGURE 12</u>

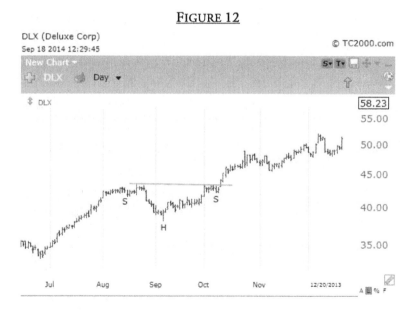

Deluxe's stock had been in a sustained uptrend for two months when the stock paused (left shoulder), declined and then increased again (head), and paused and dipped again (right shoulder) before shooting up (breakout). The result was a well-defined continuation H&S bottom. Note the horizontal neckline, abbreviated right shoulder (breakouts from which can lead to powerful trends), and a clean decisive breakout through the neckline.

All trends, up or down, pause at some point. The pause can take the form of price gyrations that do not form any classical pattern. Or the pause can be in the form of price action that evolves into a classical pattern. And that classical pattern can be either a continuation pattern that continues the previous trend or a reversal pattern that reverses the previous trend. In Deluxe Corp., the pause formed a continuation pattern in the form of a continuation H&S bottom.

Thus, when I see a stock in a sustained trend, I wait for the inevitable pause because that pause can take the form a tradable classical pattern that gives me an entry opportunity. Before, I used to ignore stocks in sustained trends because I thought, "I missed that breakout. Nothing I can do here." It is smart to not chase breakouts. My mistake was failing to realize that every chart can form a compelling set-up at any time, even after making a strong run.

We have to accept the fact that we will miss many good trades. In fact, we must not try to find and trade every compelling set-up. We need to concentrate when trading, and we should not spread our attention and capital too thin. Most importantly, we have to remember that money we did not make is not money we lost. Missing a breakout or choosing one pattern that later fails over another that turns out to be a big winner is part of trading. Nobody knew which patterns would work. It is foolish to get angry over something that we have no control over. It is far better to miss a trade than to lose money.

Note: not every price move is due to a breakout from a classical pattern. Strong trends start without any connection to a classical pattern. As classical chartists, we don't buy shares just because a stock is going up or short shares just because the stock is going down. We look for tradable classical patterns that provide favorable entry spots.

Flotek Industries: 6-week continuation H&S bottom

Here, a breakout from a 6-week H&S bottom was part of a price action that also broke above a multi-month declining resistance line:

FIGURE 13

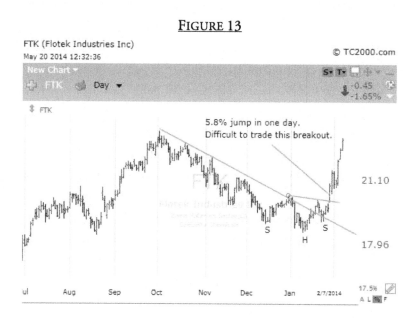

As Flotek was in a steady downtrend from October 2013 to January 2014, we might call this pattern a reversal H&S bottom. But as Flotek had been in a year-long uptrend before this recent decline, it is also reasonable to label this pattern a continuation H&S bottom. The label is unimportant. The important thing is whether a pattern offers an advantageous entry spot with a favorable reward-to-risk possibility.

Note the powerful breakout from the 6-week H&S bottom as prices jumped 5.8% on the breakout day. Buying shares toward the close of the breakout meant risking more of our position than required for most of the patterns we have examined so far. Still, trading this breakout would have been a reasonable decision, especially if we decided to use a smaller position to make sure we stayed below our maximum risk. Not trading this breakout was also a reasonable decision as there will be many more set-ups with less risky entry points.

We could have anticipated the breakout and placed a buy-stop order just above the H&S bottom's neckline. Here, such a buy-stop order would have worked well. But remember that every situation is different and that buy-stop orders do not always work to our advantage. We discussed how they can produce bigger-than-expected losses if prices jump overnight and then reverse and trigger our stop.

We cannot and should not trade every breakout. Our task is to learn the many variations in classical patterns and figure out the kinds of set-ups that we like. Classical charting does not have too many fundamental principles. But countless interesting possibilities arise from the relatively-few bedrock guidelines. We are free to use our imagination and discipline to apply classical charting in ways that we prefer if we keep risk management as our top priority. Trading is in some ways the ultimate freedom. Isn't that a big part of why we are interested in trading?

Taser International Inc.: 9-month continuation H&S bottom

Taser International's stock had more than doubled in six months and then started to trade in a range for nine months starting in late 2012. It turned out that during these nine months the stock was building a base from which to launch another powerful uptrend. The base was the following 9-month continuation H&S bottom:

FIGURE 14

Another pattern within a pattern. The right shoulder developed in the form of a descending flag. The breakout from the flag started the breakout from the larger H&S bottom pattern.

Let's zoom in on the right shoulder:

FIGURE 14.1

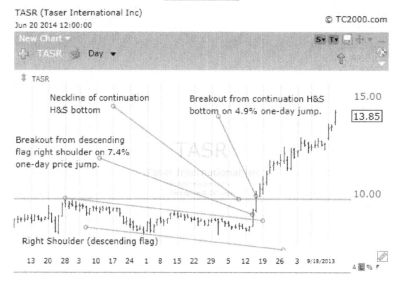

Note the unmistakable increase in volume at breakout as indicated on Figure 14. While breakout on heavy volume can never guarantee the pattern's ultimate success, it is a strong indicator of a significant breakout from a meaningful boundary.

This set-up also produced a fast breakout. Let's say we had been monitoring this pattern develop and saw the breakout from the right shoulder. Towards the end of the breakout day, we see that entering around what was going to be the closing price meant that we had to risk almost 7.5% of our position. And a possible 7.5% loss on a normal-size position is likely to exceed our maximum-loss limit for a single trade. On other hand, the pattern looks very promising and the heavy-volume confirmation on breakout makes the pattern even more enticing. What can we do?

While there is nothing wrong with not trading a breakout because, for example, we feel entering the trade means chasing a breakout, we can always consider using a smaller position. Using a smaller position helps us trade with less emotion and thus correctly. A smaller position allows us to set our stop-loss order at a more logical level: reasonably far away from the breakout boundary to give our position a reasonable chance to survive normal volatility and possible retests while still keeping our potential loss under our maximum-loss limit. Always consider whether we can use a smaller position to trade a promising pattern that has experienced an explosive breakout.

CHAPTER 8
Rectangle

Our next pattern is the humble rectangle.

<u>Chiquita Brands: 3-month rectangle</u>

Here is our first rectangle:

FIGURE 15

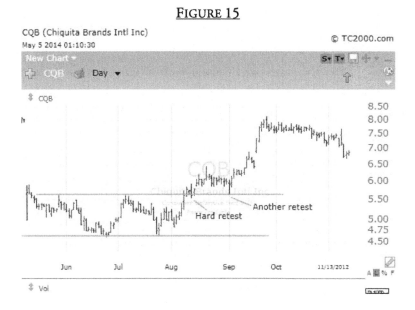

Let's focus on the breakout area:

BRIAN B. KIM

FIGURE 15.1

CQB (Chiquita Brands Intl Inc)
Jun 20 2014 12:00:00
© TC2000.com

Breakout day. High was 5.84 and low was 5.59. The first hard retest would have triggered a stop placed just below the low.

First hard retest. Low price was 5.56.

Second retest. Low of 5.63.

Even the simplest-looking pattern and breakout offer trading challenges. Note the somewhat indecisive breakout with multiple retests of the upper boundary. The first retest was especially tricky because it would have triggered a stop-loss order that was placed just below the low of the breakout day. Here, placing our stop using the last day rule was problematic because the breakout day had very little price action below the upper boundary of the rectangle. A stop-loss order placed just below the low of the breakout was simply very close to the breakout boundary and exposed to getting triggered on retests and even normal volatility.

What are our options?

We could have set our stop a bit lower, say, just below the opening price of the day before the breakout or even further down and reduce our position size accordingly to stay within our risk parameters.

Another option is to re-enter this trade if we got stopped out. If we got stopped out after placing a stop at, for example, 5.57, then we could re-enter on the day after the first retest and place a stop just below the low of the hard retest, say, at 5.54. There is no guarantee that this second stop will survive. We are simply placing our stop at a spot that seems to have a

68

reasonable chance of surviving volatility while staying within our risk limit. Risk management, not making money, must remain our priority, especially when making multiple attempts at a set-up. Here, the second stop-loss order would have survived the second retest that came three weeks later. I will always consider re-entering a trade if I am stopped out by a retest where prices do not decisively close below the breakout boundary. Sometimes I will enter for the third time if the pattern seems promising enough and I have suffered negligible losses on my initial attempts. That said, becoming fixated on any pattern because we think a pattern "owes" us is dangerous and unnecessary. There will always be other set-ups to trade. We should almost always move on after two attempts.

A crucial takeaway from Chiquita's chart is that we must expect retests, and we must learn to deal with them. One of the best ways to deal with retests is to ignore them. That is, we enter at an advantageous spot, place our stop at a reasonable level, and we move on. Anxiously watching every price tick in fear that our stop will get triggered will lead to mental exhaustion, and when we trade while tired, large losses are not far away. Perhaps an even more important lesson is that we must be patient and give the pattern time to work. After buying shares and setting our stop, we had to be patient through two hard retests over three weeks. The stock started to make big gains five weeks after breakout.

The Chiquita chart also shows the importance of detachment. The ideal way to trade is to dispassionately enter and set a stop and then do other things. Agonizing over whether our stop will survive a retest is the worst thing we can do. If our stop is triggered, so be it. We consider re-entering if practical and advantageous to do so. If we decide not to re-enter, then we move on.

Lions Gate Entertainment: 6-week rectangle

FIGURE 16

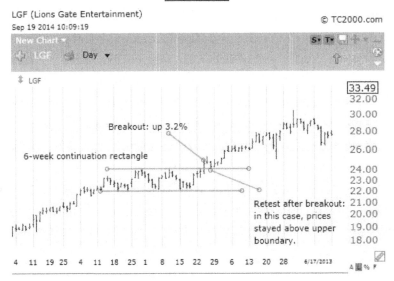

After the decisive breakout, a retest challenged but did not penetrate the upper boundary of the rectangle. It is fascinating how often pattern boundaries turn back retests. But we must not get overconfident and assume the inviolability of boundaries. The market does not care where or how we draw boundaries. Decisive breakouts can be followed by tough retests that penetrate deep inside the pattern and, of course, even lead to pattern failures. No matter how decisive and indisputable a breakout looks, we must always stay within our risk parameters and enter a stop-loss order as soon as we enter every trade.

A pattern is almost always open to multiple interpretations

I think we had two compelling ways to interpret the following chart of Lincoln National. The first interpretation of the price action is a breakout from a rectangle:

FIGURE 17

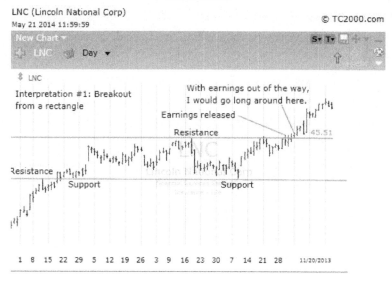

The other interpretation is a breakout from a continuation H&S bottom:

FIGURE 17.1

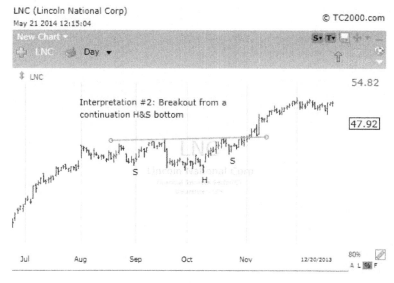

Note the abbreviated right shoulder, which can signal a potentially powerful move to come, and the slightly rising neckline.

Both interpretations are compelling and provide a clear entry and exit strategy.

A caution regarding the freedom we have in drawing boundaries and interpreting charts: we must not impose our wishes onto charts by drawing lines that reflect our hopes rather than the price action. In a battle of wills, the market will always win.

Let's examine a third way to interpret Lincoln National's chart, that of a broadening triangle, also called a megaphone, to emphasize the point that chart patterns are simply trading and risk-management tools:

FIGURE 17.2

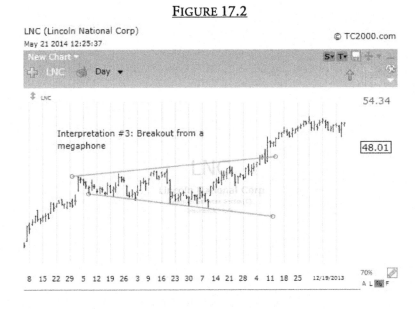

A megaphone is usually a bearish chart pattern where prices decline after breaking below the lower boundary. But prices do not have to respect our boundaries or expectations. All classical patterns can launch a powerful move in the direction opposite the expected direction. The megaphone, as it did here, can launch a powerful uptrend after prices decisively close above the upper boundary.

A lesson is that we must always keep an open mind rather than being obsessed with a particular outcome – our preferred outcome. All of us will at times fight, with no success, the price action. We do not want to and cannot believe what we are seeing because the price action is doing something that it is "not supposed" to do. In a battle between our fantasy and reality, guess which side wins?

If we remained flexible, we were much more likely to spot and trade well a breakout either way. Spotting a pattern and the breakout are only part of trading well. We need to determine a good entry and exit strategy that manages risk. And the megaphone interpretation simply did not give us as favorable a trading strategy as the rectangle and continuation H&S bottom interpretations. It was not impossible to trade this breakout well on the basis of a megaphone interpretation. But the rectangle and continuation H&S bottom interpretations provided clearer and more favorable entry and exit points because of modest differences in the drawing of the pattern boundary. We could enter the trade a bit earlier using the rectangle and continuation H&S bottom interpretations and also benefit from their horizontal or nearly horizontal breakout boundaries. As we will discuss further later, patterns with horizontal boundaries offer some advantages over slanting boundaries to traders.

Skechers: 4-month rectangle

One more rectangle:

FIGURE 18

SKX (Skechers Usa Inc)
Sep 19 2014 10:17:39
© TC2000.com

Approximate price target: 26.30.
With the price target met and the
earnings report coming up, I would
sell my entire position here.

Earnings released

Breakout

The breakout was clear and gave traders plenty of time to enter. We could buy shares towards the close of the breakout day and even the next day and stay within our risk parameters. And note that the minimum price target was quickly met. While the general rule is that a measured price target is usually the minimum price move, it is also true that at anytime prices can reverse and lead to pattern failure. I almost always take profits on most of my position when a price target is met. When, as here, the price target is met and the next quarterly earnings report is due soon, I will exit entirely from my position.

CHAPTER 9
Ascending Triangle

The ascending triangle is a pattern that indicates a possible upward price move. It has a horizontal top boundary and a rising lower boundary with increasingly higher lows.

<u>Marchex Inc.: 10-month ascending triangle</u>

FIGURE 19

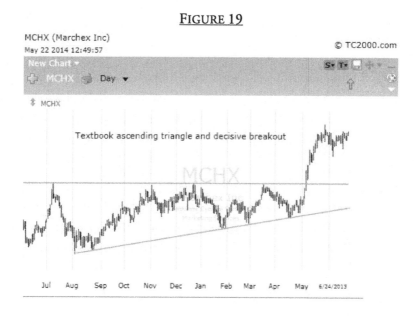

The next chart focuses on the breakout area:

FIGURE 19.1

MCHX (Marchex Inc)
Jun 23 2014 01:07:20
© TC2000.com

MCHX
Powerful but difficult-to-trade breakout: up 8.5% in one day. One option is
placing a buy-stop order in anticipation of a breakout. Another option
is buying a smaller-than-normal position.

Upper boundary of
ascending triangle.

Higher volume on up days and breakout

One of the ironies of trading is that an explosive breakout both confirms
the significance of the pattern and makes trading the pattern more difficult.
The powerful breakout in Marchex is an example. Placing a buy-stop order
in anticipation of a breakout would have worked well in this case, but
remember that a stop order to buy or short is not a perfect tool.

We face a tricky situation here. We know in hindsight that Marchex
went on a powerful run after breaking out of the ascending triangle. In
hindsight it is easy to say, "we should have bought a large position after
breakout." But we trade in real time, and in real time the dilemma was
whether to buy shares on the breakout day and risk up to 10% of our
position. Another factor to consider was the fact that Marchex was a
relatively thinly-traded stock. So we had a powerful breakout from a
textbook pattern in a low-volume and volatile stock. What are some of our
options?

First, we can simply not trade. It is better to miss a trade than to chase a
breakout and lose money. Let it go. There will be others.

Second, we could have placed a buy-stop order in anticipation of a
breakout. This option is no longer available after breakout but it is still
worth mentioning because buy-stop orders can be a valuable tool especially

if we learn to use a smaller position size to account for a possible gap up in price. Again, buy-stop orders are not foolproof and can produce bigger-than-expected losses.

Third, we can buy a smaller-than-normal position at around the closing price.

There is no correct choice among these options. Sometimes one option will work better while other times a different choice will produce the better outcome. Whatever option we choose, we must be guided by our most important objective: controlling risk and cutting losses.

Cheesecake Factory: 3-month ascending triangle

The next chart shows a well-formed ascending triangle in Cheesecake Factory from July to October 2013:

FIGURE 20

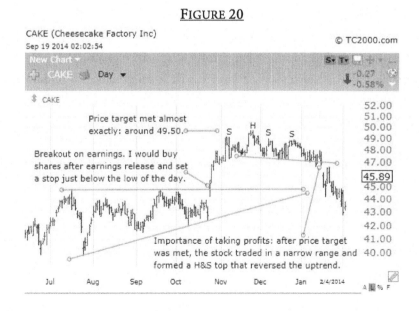

Sometimes the earnings-induced breakout is so powerful that it puts the trade out of our reach. Other times the earnings news will produce a decisive yet manageable breakout that provides a favorable entry spot, as happened in this ascending triangle. We could have bought shares around the breakout day's closing price and set a stop just below the breakout day's low.

Note the earnings news led to a breakout on a gap up in price. Not all price gaps are significant, but price gaps that overcome key resistance or support levels are often decisive clues.

After breakout, the stock reached its measured price target, which is the height of the ascending triangle as its widest point – here, $5 – projected upward from the breakout level. The price target was met on the dot. I almost always take profits at the measured price target. Although price targets are generally minimum price goals, I still exit most of my position when targets are reached. If prices continue to go up or down and leave us behind, then so what? We bank our profits and move on to other set-ups.

After reaching the price target, Cheesecake's stock price went sideways for two months before breaking down. Note that the stock formed a 2-month H&S top from which the decline started.

Some takeaways from Cheesecake's chart:

First, the importance of taking profits when the measured price target is reached. Many good traders say that it is the sitting on our position, never our thinking, that makes the big money. This idea can work well, especially in powerful bull markets, but as with everything, not always. Depending on market conditions, I may take profits well before the price target is reached.

Second, again, we must not gamble on earnings releases by entering a large position just before earnings news.

Lastly, in this case there was an attractive entry point even after the powerful breakout on earnings. As we noted, most trades, including many of the best trades, give us plenty of time to enter. They key is to be not mentally and financially exhausted when the fat pitch is served.

Dollar Tree Stores: 8-week ascending triangle

Here is another breakout on a gap up in price:

FIGURE 21

DLTR (Dollar Tree Stores Inc)
Oct 3 2014 12:00:00
© TC2000.com

Price target met

Breakout day closing
price: 55.86

4.5% drop on
earnings news

Closing price on day before
breakout: 54.87

Interpretation #1:
Ascending triangle

Such a "breakout gap," the same one we saw in Cheesecake Factory's ascending triangle in Figure 20, is more often than not evidence of a meaningful breakout.

Also notice that we need to modify the last day rule to set our stop here. Because of the gap up, there was no price action within the pattern on the breakout day. One alternative is to set a stop just below the closing price of the day before the breakout. Or, if within our risk parameter, we can set our stop below the low price of the day before. Every stop placement will depend on the particular traits of each pattern. Here, the breakout on a gap up was not so powerful as to make buying shares too risky.

After reaching the price target, prices traded in a narrow range until the quarterly earnings report. Again, I would have exited from my entire position before the earnings release. Here, the stock price dropped sharply on earnings news.

Dollar Tree Stores: Was that a continuation H&S bottom instead?

Is it possible to interpret Figure 21 in a different way? The following chart shows how we could have interpreted it as a continuation H&S bottom:

FIGURE 21.1

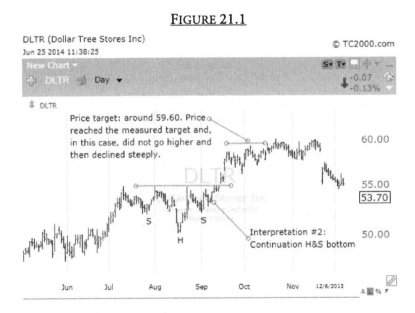

How we interpret and label the price action is up to each of us. We could call this chart an upside down Mt. Everest. What is not debatable is the importance of risk management and limiting losses.

Michael Kors Holding: 5-month ascending triangle

The next ascending triangle developed a symmetrical triangle inside its boundaries:

FIGURE 22

The next chart zooms in on the breakout area:

FIGURE 22.1

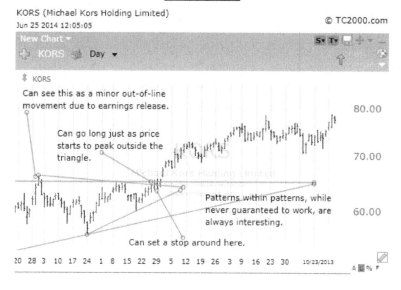

I am always interested in a pattern-within-a-pattern because it often provides an opportunity to enter the trade earlier than otherwise. For example, here we had a good rationale for buying shares when prices closed above the symmetrical triangle's upper boundary but before closing above the ascending triangle's upper boundary. Doing so meant buying shares two or three days earlier than had we waited for prices to close above the upper boundary of the ascending triangle. A couple of days may not seem like much but slight edges can make a big difference. Classical charting is about exploiting small edges over many trades. In this case, the advantage of entering a few days earlier was not only higher profits should the pattern work but simply securing an entry in this trade. For if we had waited for a more decisive breakout, we would find that buying shares required taking on significantly greater risk as prices gapped up three days after they initially closed above the symmetrical triangle's upper boundary.

Caution: the chance of being left behind is never a good reason to enter a trade. Here, I think the breakout from the symmetrical triangle was a good spot to buy shares. That said, I also think waiting for a more decisive breakout from both the smaller symmetrical triangle and larger ascending triangle was a reasonable decision. We could not know that prices would gap up three days after they broke out of the symmetrical triangle. Even after the gap up, we could buy a smaller position to enter this trade and stay within our risk parameters. Or we could decide to trade other set-ups instead. There will always be others.

Nu Skin Enterprises: 7-week ascending triangle

Nu Skin Enterprises formed an ascending triangle from May to July 2013:

FIGURE 23

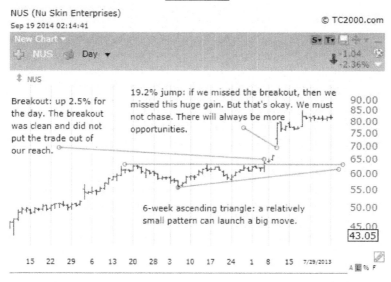

The breakout from the ascending triangle was clear enough but not explosive. I like such a "controlled breakout" because it almost always creates a favorable entry spot that doesn't ask us to risk too much of our position. Prices steadily moved higher the next two days and then jumped 20% on the third day after the breakout. Prices paused for a week before moving higher again. This simple 7-week pattern produced a 30% profit in two weeks. A lesson is that we should not place too much emphasis on spotting and trading the giant multi-month or multi-year patterns. Relatively small patterns like this ascending triangle that form after a powerful run (Nu Skin stock had gone up more than 50% in the three months prior to forming this ascending triangle) often launch another powerful run. These modest but potentially powerful patterns are called halfway continuation patterns because they often form at about the midpoint of the overall move.

Sealed Air Corp.: 14-week ascending triangle

We have a decisive breakout from a well-defined ascending triangle:

FIGURE 24

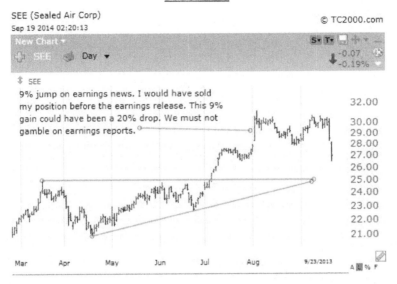

SEE (Sealed Air Corp)

Sep 19 2014 02:20:13

© TC2000.com

New Chart ▾

SEE Day ▾

-0.07
-0.19%

$ SEE

9% jump on earnings news. I would have sold my position before the earnings release. This 9% gain could have been a 20% drop. We must not gamble on earnings reports.

32.00
30.00
29.00
28.00
27.00
26.00
25.00
24.00
23.00
22.00
21.00

Mar   Apr   May   Jun   Jul   Aug   9/23/2013

A ▣ % F

The stock is making a good run and seems poised to reach its measured price target. But the next earnings report is to be released soon. What should we do?

My opinion is that we should sell our shares rather than stay in and hope that the market reacts positively to the earnings report. If we must stay in, despite nothing and no one forcing us to hold our shares through an earnings release, then we should gamble with just a small portion of our original position, say, no more than 20% to 30%.

What we must not do is keep our full position because the stock price "should" and "must" reach its measured price target. No. Wrong. Never. There are no such guarantees in the markets. Measured price targets are just possibilities. They serve as useful reference points but never as scientific certainties. The market doesn't care what the price target is. How the market reacts to earnings news is entirely unpredictable. The only certainty is uncertainty. It is a highly unoriginal statement, but it is true, and often forgotten. Good earnings can be seen as bad while bad can be good. Or, good can be not quite good enough and thus bad but the stock price may skyrocket anyway. Or crash. Nobody knows. We must not gamble on earnings reports.

Sealed Air Corp.: was Figure 24 a symmetrical triangle and not an ascending triangle?

Some of us may object that it is more accurate to draw and label the Sealed Air Corp. chart as a symmetrical triangle as follows:

FIGURE 24.1

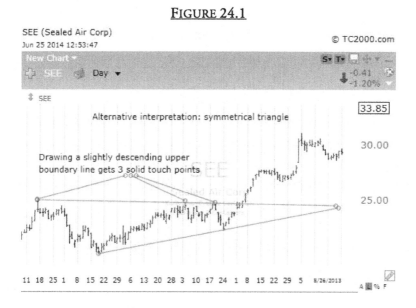

Drawing our boundary as an ascending triangle meant a horizontal upper boundary with only one price touch point. There were two other price peaks that came close to the upper boundary. In contrast, interpreting this 14-week pattern as a symmetrical triangle and drawing a slightly descending upper boundary created an upper boundary with three solid price touches. More touches on a boundary are good. Then is there a reasonable basis for interpreting this pattern as an ascending triangle?

First, the two highs came close enough to the upper boundary for it to be reasonable to label this chart as an ascending triangle. Remember that patterns do not have to be perfect to be useful. Pattern boundaries are just lines that we draw and use as trading tools and nothing more. There is no rule that says that prices must stay within their "proper" (our) boundaries. Prices will go wherever they want to go. While it is fascinating to observe how often prices do stay within the lines that we draw, we must never forget that prices can run over our lines anytime. It can be costly to draw very precise pattern boundaries because we then expect and demand prices to respect these sacred lines. We become too invested in the inviolability of our chosen boundary. And when prices violate our lines, we go into denial and become blind to the actual price action.

Second, some traders will say, with merit, that whatever we call this pattern, a breakout of significance will have to close decisively above a meaningful resistance level. Here, the upper boundary of the ascending triangle was such a level because that line represents the highest price reached within the pattern and a level of resistance that has rejected three attempts to overcome it. So some traders will say fine, we'll call this pattern a symmetrical triangle if you wish, but a breakout from a symmetrical triangle is not a true breakout until it closes above a significant prior high.

The next example illustrates this point.

Spring Nextel Corp.: 6-month symmetrical triangle

Let's see how this set-up illustrates the previous point. First, the big-picture view:

FIGURE 25

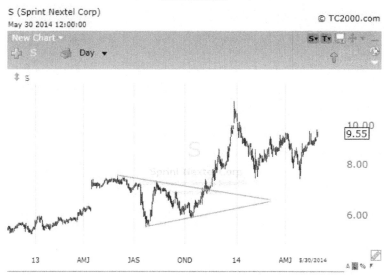

The next chart focuses on the second half of the symmetrical triangle:

FIGURE 25.1

And the next chart zooms in on the breakout area:

FIGURE 25.2

The stock closed above the symmetrical triangle's upper boundary but was turned back on its first attempt to close above the horizontal resistance formed by the previous significant high. The rejection led to a hard retest where prices traded but not close below the upper boundary of the symmetrical triangle. Another, some would say the real, breakout came eight days later when the stock decisively cleared the horizontal resistance level. Some will argue that the initial close above the upper boundary of the symmetrical triangle was a good entry signal. After all, a stop placed at a reasonable distance away from the boundary would have survived even the hard retest. A long position entered at the initial breakout would have meant an earlier and thus more profitable entry. This analysis, too, has merit.

I think we should incorporate the wisdom of both sides in our trading. Breakouts are about overcoming key resistance and support levels. While sloping lines can be precise resistance and support levels, horizontal lines present the clearest picture of support and resistance. But charting is also about exploiting small edges, and we may prefer to enter a bit earlier as signaled by the symmetrical triangle interpretation. After all, a failed breakout means just a minor loss while a successful breakout means we have a running start.

Symetra Financial Corp.: 4-month ascending triangle

Our last ascending triangle shows the upper boundary offering stiff resistance against multiple breakout attempts:

FIGURE 26

The many decisive breakouts we have analyzed so far may give us the impression that all breakouts are very clean and easy to trade. This impression is false and dangerous. While it is true that many of the best trades start with clean breakouts, some struggle to get going.

In Figure 26, the congestion at the upper boundary that seems like nothing in hindsight lasted a week. We have to accept the fact that not all breakouts will be clean. All we can do is enter and set our stop at a spot that limits our risk. If we get stopped out, no problem. If the trade starts to work, we find out when the next earnings report is due and where we might take profits. Whatever happens, we move on to other set-ups. There are always more opportunities to be found.

CHAPTER 10
Descending Triangle

Our next pattern is the descending triangle, which indicates a possible downward move in prices. It has a flat lower boundary and descending upper boundary with lower highs.

<u>Caesars Entertainment: 4-week descending triangle</u>

Our first descending triangle is small but well-defined:

FIGURE 27

The breakdown through the lower horizontal boundary was decisive. When the measured price target was reached in a week, I would cover my entire position. Then came a retest where the stock nearly reached the lower boundary of the descending triangle. If we missed the initial breakout, the retest offered a second chance to enter a short trade.

A note of caution: I almost always use a smaller position when entering a trade in a stock that has already reached its price target and then has returned to retest the breakout boundary. My rationale is that the pattern breakout has already served its purpose. This situation is different from the common and expected retest that occurs within a few days or a few weeks of a breakout and where prices have yet to make significant progress toward the price target.

With Caesars Entertainment, shorting again or for the first time just under the lower boundary during the retest level would have worked well as prices again declined. Note the upcoming quarterly earnings release and the caution we must exercise by covering our short position and getting out of this trade.

NutriSystem Inc.: 4-month descending triangle

An upcoming earnings release again affects our trading in the next example:

FIGURE 28

NutriSystem formed a textbook descending triangle. After a decisive downward breakout, the downtrend paused and prices traded within a narrow range for a week until the earnings report. If we had shorted shares after the breakout, we would cover our shares before the earnings release. Prices declined 12% on the earnings news and then declined another 12% in the following days. Yes, we would have made a large profit if we had stayed with our short position. But I have no doubt that staying in our short position would have been the wrong thing to do. We have to remember that while doing the right thing, which should be our definition of trading well, does not guarantee a profit, it does dramatically increase our chances of preserving our capital. In contrast, doing the wrong thing by taking on too much risk or gambling on earnings can sometimes lead to large profits but it dramatically increases the odds of crippling losses. Nobody knew how the market would react to the earnings report. That 12% decline could have been a 20% or even a 40% increase.

The following are some questions we might have about this set-up.

First, since the next earnings report was due a week after the breakout, should we have traded this breakout? My opinion is that we should consider trading every decisive breakout, including a breakout very close to the next earnings report, because prices can travel far in a short time. For example, it was very possible for NutriSystem's stock, after breaking down through the lower horizontal boundary of the descending triangle, to decline another, say, 10% to 20% in the days leading up to the earnings release. If this decline had occurred, then we would cover our short position before the earnings release and book a significant profit. A week and perhaps even a couple of days is enough time for a stock to make a significant move in the anticipated direction to make breakouts in situations like NutriSystem's worth trading.

Second, was the breakdown from the descending triangle in anticipation of a bad earnings report? Some traders and investors made a bet on the basis of their opinion or guess that the market would react negatively to earnings, but no one knew for certain. It is obvious but worth repeating: no one and no chart knows the future direction of stock prices.

We must not risk our precious capital on the utterances of those who claim to know something. I think it is a common mistake to think that those in Wall Street know, or at least have a better idea of, the future. The same caution must be applied to our charts, especially with a breakout from a pattern just before an earnings release as we are tempted to think that the price action must be reflective of somebody knowing something and is a reliable forecast of the future. The market can coldly reverse a decisive breakout anytime it wishes and produce outright pattern failure.

A third question may be: if NutriSystem's stock increased on earnings news, then wouldn't our stop be triggered and we would be out of our position with just a small loss? So isn't it a win-win strategy to stay in our short position? If the price continues to decline, then we profit. If the price goes up, then we get stopped out for a small loss.

My response is that if it were guaranteed that our stop would be triggered at exactly or near where we placed our stop, then yes, staying in our short position through the earnings release is the dominant strategy. **But there are no such guarantees in trading**. While the stock gapped down on earnings news, it could have gapped up just as easily. And the gap up could have been huge. I've seen price gaps measuring 20% to 40% and more. And even larger gaps have happened and will happen. By getting out of our position before the earnings release, we avoid this immeasurable, unpredictable, and unnecessary risk.

Let's review. We should not hold a position through an earnings release, no matter how promising the chart pattern and how clean the breakout. The only time I will seriously consider holding a very small position through earnings is if I am sitting on a significant profit. Even a reduced exposure does not guarantee that we will make money in the trade. The profit that we made when we exited most of our position may turn into an overall loss if prices gap in the direction opposite the anticipated direction. We may even suffer a very large loss if the price gap is large enough.

The only guarantee in trading is that we will suffer psychologically and financially if we don't respect risk. Our priority is protecting our capital. An intact trading account allows us to take advantage of favorable market conditions and highly advantageous set-ups.

CHAPTER 11
Symmetrical Triangle

Unlike ascending or descending triangles, symmetrical triangles do not indicate the likely direction of the breakout because both the upper and lower boundaries converge to an apex. Thus, prices can break up or down. Still, I would say that most symmetrical triangles are continuation patterns that continue the previous trend.

Chicago Bridge & Iron: 4-month symmetrical triangle

The first symmetrical triangle we will look at formed in Chicago Bridge & Iron from May to September 2013. It had textbook form and produced a clean and decisive breakout:

FIGURE 29

This textbook symmetrical triangle was one of the most meaningful classical patterns for me in 2013.

Why?

Because I did not trade the breakout despite having watched the pattern develop for months. I did not trade the breakout because I did not believe the breakout. I saw the breakout, but I didn't believe anything would come from it.

Why?

The stock had made an incredible run and was just under the old high set before the financial crisis of 2007-2009. I thought that the uptrend was surely over. Even the humble old-industry name of the company contributed to my inaction. Could such a heavy-sounding name continue to go up? Of course nobody knew that the stock would make another powerful run after the decisive breakout from this 4-month symmetrical triangle. Not knowing the future was not my mistake. My mistake was ignoring the breakout and eliminating the pattern from trade consideration because the stock was doing something that I didn't want it to do and couldn't believe it could do: continue to go up.

This humble, textbook symmetrical triangle reminded me, again, that my job as a trader is to believe what I see, what the price is doing, rather than believe what I want to believe or what "should" happen. Spot a pattern, observe the breakout, enter if there is a favorable entry point, and place a stop that limits the potential loss. Then move on to other charts. Repeat.

Here, we would have risked less than 3% of our position to enter a promising trade by buying shares at the closing price of the breakout day, $62.98, and setting our stop just below the low at, for example, $61.11. Yet I did not take a swing at this set-up because I refused to accept what my eyes were telling me: a decisive breakout from a textbook symmetrical triangle. We'll talk more about Chicago Bridge & Iron's chart in Chapter 21.

Central European Media: 3-month reversal symmetrical triangle

A reversal symmetrical triangle reverses the previous trend. The reversal symmetrical triangle in CETV featured a textbook shape and a hard retest after breakout:

FIGURE 30

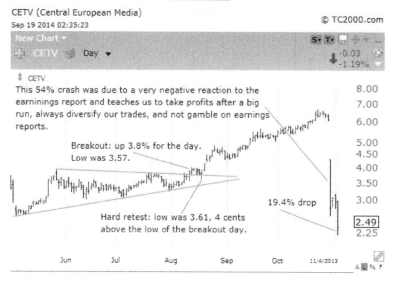

CETV (Central European Media)
Sep 19 2014 02:35:23
© TC2000.com

This 54% crash was due to a very negative reaction to the earninings report and teaches us to take profits after a big run, always diversify our trades, and not gamble on earnings reports.

Breakout: up 3.8% for the day.
Low was 3.57.

Hard retest: low was 3.61, 4 cents above the low of the breakout day.

19.4% drop

From May to August 2013, Central European Media formed a textbook 5-point reversal symmetrical triangle. The pattern formed after a steep multi-year decline in which the stock lost more than 90% of its value.

Prices closed above the upper boundary on August 12. For the next four days prices retested but did not trade below the upper boundary. On the fifth day there was a hard retest where the stock price penetrated the upper boundary and traded as low as $3.61. This hard retest was tricky but also supported the idea that the initial breakout had significance because even this deep retest would not have triggered a stop-loss order set just below the low of the breakout day. Also, prices reversed and closed above the upper boundary by the end of the day of the hard retest.

If we had already bought shares after the August 12 breakout, we could consider adding a modest position to our original position after the hard retest. If we had not yet entered this trade, the retest day was a good time to enter while setting a stop just below the low of the retest. Prices jumped 8.4% the next day and surged higher for the next 2 months.

This example is a good trade but also a set-up that we had to be extra careful with for several reasons.

While CETV was not a low-volume stock, it is a low-price and very volatile stock. Extra caution is warranted if we choose to trade such stocks. It is a good idea to use a smaller position in this situation. It is also perfectly fine to avoid stocks trading under a certain dollar amount no matter how promising the patterns they are forming. We have to remember that there will always be more great set-ups. Look again at the symmetrical triangle that formed in Chicago Bridge & Iron in Figure 29 – a humble name, an old-school industry, a textbook pattern, a clear breakout, and not even a retest of any kind to deal with. Never forget: there will always, always, always be other opportunities.

We might have guessed what our next point of caution is. Our good friend the quarterly earnings report. How many times have we said that we shouldn't gamble on earnings reports? CETV's powerful uptrend was annihilated by a bad earnings report. The stock dropped 54% in one day.

There are so many basic lessons to be repeated here. Never bet our entire trading account on one stock. Take profits on all or at least most of our position when the measured price target is reached. Gamble with just a small slice of our original position if we decide to take an unnecessary gamble on an earnings release. Let's say we were happy to sell all our shares with a 30% gain on this trade. Then who cares if the stock gains another 50% after we sold? Yes, we are human, so we will be somewhat disappointed. But the trader who is successful over the long run will take the 30% gain and move on to the next opportunity. Because there will always be more great setups.

Lastly, it was possible to interpret the CETV chart as an ascending triangle:

FIGURE 30.1

As we noted, some traders prefer to interpret a price action as a pattern with a horizontal boundary whenever reasonable to do so. Note that the initial breakout that occurred in the symmetrical triangle was not a breakout in the ascending-triangle interpretation. The decisive breakout from the ascending triangle came five trading days later.

Again, there is merit in both interpretations. The symmetrical-triangle interpretation allowed a trader to enter the trade several days earlier and the hard retest also provided a second chance to enter. The ascending-triangle interpretation signalled the trader to wait for a more significant breakout because it was the 8.4% price jump that decisively closed above a significant prior high within the pattern. The interpretive choice is ours depending on our temperament and trading style. Whichever interpretation we choose, we must stay under our maximum risk with our entry and exit points.

Chiquita Brands: 4-month symmetrical triangle

We have another well-shaped symmetrical triangle:

FIGURE 31

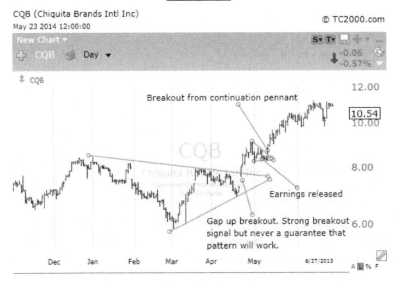

Note that the breakout came on a large gap up in price. Let's zoom in on the breakout area:

FIGURE 31.1

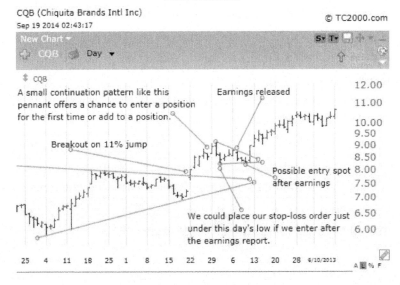

We saw how powerful breakouts, while exciting and possibly indicating a big move to come, can make entering the trade difficult or inadvisable by forcing us to risk a larger percentage of our position than we would like. For example, here, the breakout came on a 11% one-day jump. Fortunately, we didn't have to risk 11% of our position to enter this trade. Even entering around the closing price of the breakout day and setting our stop just below the low price of the breakout day meant risking under 5% of our position. The specific price action in every breakout will be different and, in this case, there was significant trading within the pattern boundary on the breakout day to give reasonable cushion to a stop placed just below the low of the day. While this stop could still get hit by a hard retest, the stop was reasonably far away from the pattern boundary and the closing price to make, in my mind, the trade a worthwhile risk.

Prices increased another 10% in the days after the breakout. Then the stock paused. And the next quarterly earnings report was due to be released within a week. I would sell my entire position before the earnings release and book a significant profit. I would also continue to monitor this chart. We don't need to check every hour. A quick but focused look once a day is sufficient to spot interesting developments. The stock neither surged up nor broke down in response to the earnings report. Instead, the stock continued to trade within a narrow range.

This range-bound action was potentially significant because small continuation patterns such as pennants (small symmetrical triangles) and flags (small rectangles or parallelograms) can form after the initial breakout. The fact that Chiquita's stock traded within a relatively narrow range in the days leading up to the earnings report and continued to do so in the days following gave rise to the possibility that a continuation pennant or flag was forming. Pennants and flags are by definition, given their small size, patterns with narrow price fluctuations.

The range-bound price action was also significant because it offered an advantageous place to enter an anticipatory trade. I say anticipatory because there was not yet a decisive breakout from a well-formed pennant or flag. I do not usually enter anticipatory trades and I think classical chartists should mostly trade breakouts from classical patterns. Still, there is value to considering different ways to apply classical charting principles. We can adopt only those methods that we feel comfortable with. Here, we could consider entering an anticipatory trade because a low-risk entry spot arose two days after the earnings release when the stock closed a little above the retest low. If we were to buy shares at this point, and if the stock price subsequently declined below the lowest point of the retest, then we would be stopped out for a very small loss barring any price gaps down. Instead, the stock price jumped 7.9% next day and broke out of a 2-week pennant. Of course nobody knew the stock would jump nearly 8%. And some of us may feel that anticipatory trades, including this one, blur the line between disciplined trading of clear breakouts and random trading. But others may decide to make this anticipatory trade because they saw a small edge. There is no single correct way to trade. We can choose a style that suits us best.

It is sometimes the case with small continuation patterns like this pennant that we see the pattern only after the breakout. Hence the usefulness of an exploratory position that tries to anticipate a breakout. My guess is that most of us would not have entered an anticipatory position, and that is fine. I think it would have been reasonable to buy a smaller than usual position even after the 7.9% breakout. With the earnings release out of the way and a decisive breakout from a pennant, entering a smaller position that kept our potential loss under our maximum risk was a worthwhile trade to make.

One last word on anticipatory trades. I hesitated discussing such entries because they can lead us away from the discipline and strict risk management that are so important to long-term survival and profitability. We may get the idea that we have a good excuse to take larger and reckless risks in the name of anticipating a breakout. This danger is why I repeat again and again, and will repeat again and again, that every trade we enter must be at a spot on the chart that offers an advantageous reward-to-risk possibility and keeps our potential loss under our maximum risk.

It is vital for us to embrace these cautionary principles and to recognize that such rules are not meant to needlessly limit our trading. **Instead,** anticipatory entries when properly done can reduce risk and increase profits. They can be the profitable outlet for disciplined creativity.

Energen Corp.: 2-year symmetrical triangle

This symmetrical triangle is one of the largest patterns in the book. Let's first look at the weekly chart as it provides a useful big-picture view of the set-up:

FIGURE 32

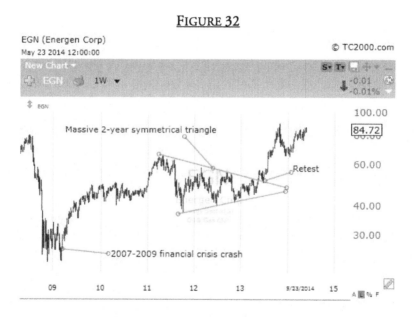

Note the crash due to the financial crisis of 2007 to 2009 when Energen, like many stocks, lost more than 50% of its value. The stock started to recover in 2009 and peaked in the early part of 2011. Then the stock made a series of lower highs and higher lows over the next two years. A giant symmetrical triangle was forming. Would the triangle launch another upward run or start a decline? Whichever way the stock broke, the size of the pattern suggested that the move could be very powerful.

I think now is a good time to remind ourselves of the importance of not getting obsessed with any set-up. Recall our discussion on how we need to trade with emotional detachment. The danger with massive multi-year patterns like this triangle is that we can get too attached to them. We imagine all the money we'll make if a mega pattern reaches its measured price target. So we might even plan to go all in. We must never try to define our trading career in a single trade. If we do, our career may end, and not in the way we hoped. Even the most promising, textbook-perfect, straight-A-plus, well-mannered, and superfood-eating pattern must be looked at in terms of the cold bottom line: is there an advantageous entry point with a favorable reward-to-risk ratio? Successful trading is about patiently implementing a repeatable process that manages risk over many trades.

Another fact we must remember: all patterns can fail any time, even after a decisive breakout that seems to confirm without any doubt the significance of the pattern. Let's say there was a decisive upward breakout from a hypothetical 3-year symmetrical triangle. We buy shares at the breakout and we are quickly up 15% on our position. We are very happy and excited. Then the stock price starts to come back down and soon retests the breakout boundary. Then the stock closes below the boundary. We are frustrated and hope our stop won't be triggered. But we are stopped out the next day. We are angry. How could this happen? There was a perfect breakout from a perfect pattern. So we enter again with a very large position without any justification. The stock continues to decline. We double our position. The stock will turn around soon. We know it. The perfect pattern won't allow us to lose money. The stock continues to crash and we lose a lot of money. The lesson is that we must not get attached to any single trade.

Trading well is not about finding perfect patterns or making money. It is doing the right thing over and over by trading only advantageous set-ups and waiting patiently when there are none.

Let's return to the Energen set-up and look at a daily chart to get a better view of the breakout:

FIGURE 32.1

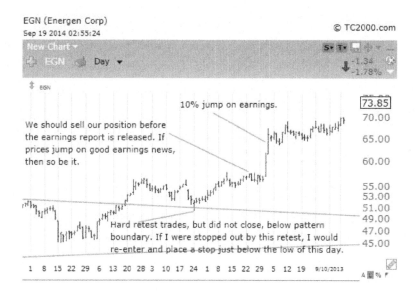

A closer look at the breakout and ensuing action shows that the breakout from this massive pattern did not lead to easy profits. It is true that the stock made steady gains for a week after breaking out. Then prices paused and traded in a choppy and somewhat downward manner for a month. That's a full month of the stock going nowhere. No easy profits so far. Then the stock declined farther to do a hard retest of the symmetrical triangle's upper boundary. During the retest, the stock price traded below but did not close below the upper boundary. This development did not guarantee that the pattern would work. But it did support the view that the upper boundary was now an important support level and that the initial breakout still had significance. The resilience of the upper boundary was good news, but the hard retest triggered stops set close to the boundary, including a stop based on the last day rule. That's no big deal. Our stop served its function and we would be out with a small loss.

The next question is whether we should re-enter this trade after getting stopped out by the hard retest. If I were stopped out by the hard retest on June 24, I would have reentered this trade around the closing price of the retest day and set my stop just below the retest low.

I would re-enter for the following reasons.

The stock price closed above the pattern boundary after the retest. And most importantly, the retest day created a favorable reward-to-risk scenario with logical entry (closing price) and exit (just below the lowest reach of the hard retest) points. Let us repeat: the fact that prices closed above the pattern boundary after the hard retest did not guarantee that the pattern would work and that there would be no further retests. But it did create an entry spot with a potentially very favorable reward-to-risk possibility. That did not mean we had to enter the trade, but if we did, it did mean that we had a justifiable reason for the trade and that any loss would be very small. If another retest triggered my stop order, then I would be out again with a small loss and I would then move on to other charts. But if the stock started to move up from here, then my position's upside potential was much greater than my potential loss barring a price gap down. The stock went up about 10% in the next month. That's a good gain, but a month of patience was required. Again, nothing easy so far.

Furthermore, we are now only days away from the quarterly earnings report. I almost always exit my entire position before the next earnings report. One exception is when I'm sitting on a substantial profit and decide to keep at most about a third of my original position through the earnings report. Here, if I had bought shares after the hard retest, I would be sitting on a 10% profit. And I may unwisely decide to risk a small portion of this profit through the earnings release. Doing so is a pure gamble. The fact that prices broke out of a mega pattern and that the pattern survived a hard retest do not predict or guarantee that the market will react positively to the earnings report. Prices will do whatever they want. In this case, the market reacted positively to the earnings report. But staying in, even with a small position, was the wrong decision and a bad trade.

Evercore Partners: 4-month symmetrical triangle

Our next example presents another situation where the earnings report was due a few weeks after the breakout:

FIGURE 33

Notice the six solid price touches with the upper and lower boundaries. Also note when the stock traded but did not close outside the lower pattern boundary. That is called an **out-of-line movement**. Remember that prices do not have to stay within our boundaries. The lines we draw allow us to visualize the price action and help us spot logical entry and stop points that keep us within our risk parameters. Patterns don't have to be perfect to be very useful trading tools.

It was possible to interpret the out-of-line movement as a breakout attempt to the downside from a 5-point reversal symmetrical triangle. And some of us may have entered a short position when prices broke down through the lower pattern boundary. If so, we would also place a buy-to-cover stop order, perhaps just above the high of the day. By the end of the trading day, however, we saw that the stock price closed back above the pattern boundary. We may have decided to exit our short position then or, if not, we would have been stopped out the next day when the stock traded above the high of what turned out to be a one-day out-of-line movement.

The loss we suffered from this unsuccessful short position would be nothing more than a minor annoyance if we used the appropriate position size. We could consider it a bet that was worth taking because the risk was well defined and limited.

Whether or not we entered a short trade due to the out-of-line movement, it was productive to continue to monitor the pattern. It was clear that prices were coiling and still possibly forming a symmetrical triangle.

The next breakout was to the upside. Had we bought shares at around the closing price of the breakout, our position would be up by about 7% by the time earnings were due to be released. That's a good gain in such a short period. It would be wise and proper to sell our entire position and move on to other patterns.

But let's assume that our emotions push us to gamble and we decide to sell two-thirds of our original position and keep one-third through the earnings release. In this case, our irresponsible and unnecessary gamble somewhat "worked" in that prices initially increased but prices soon stalled and did not go higher for a month. Had we chosen to unwisely gamble on the earnings report, we were rewarded (for our bad and risky behavior) with significant gains only if we stayed patient for several months. Prices rarely go straight up or down. They often build a foundation before starting a trend and also take frequent breaks, and some of these foundations and breaks take the form of classical patterns. **Remember that not all price moves can be explained by classical patterns. Prices go up, down, and sideways for any or no reason. Not all trends are launched by classical patterns.**

Genworth Financial: 2-month symmetrical triangle

This pattern shows again the utmost importance of patience:

FIGURE 34

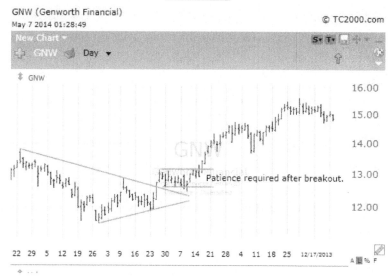

After a clean breakout, the stock stalled and traded in narrow range for 3 weeks. That's right: that little area enclosed in the small box was three weeks. It was possible to interpret this 3-week price action as a small rectangle or a continuation flag. Whatever our label, we had to wait patiently for almost a month until prices broke out of it and made large gains. If we cannot control our emotions, do not learn to relax, and do not learn to step away once we have entered a position, there is little chance that we would have had the patience and peace of mind to stay with our position until the real uptrend began.

Of course there was no guarantee that the uptrend would be so powerful, or that there would be any trend. No one could know what would follow.

This Genworth chart shows perfectly that the only things we can control are: (1) entering a trade at a favorable spot, (2) setting a stop that keeps potential losses within our risk tolerance, and (3) then turning our attention to other charts, projects, and interests. The breakout was reasonably decisive but soon stalled. Unless we accept the fact that we have no control over prices and there is nothing more we can do other than to let the pattern play out, we will fail in this trade and in trading. Each bar in that stall area represents a day. Imagine staring at our screen wondering and agonizing over whether and when the stock will continue the uptrend started by the breakout – for three weeks. We cannot do it. We can, but we'll be physically and emotionally spent in a few days. If we get exhausted, we don't have the mental and physical strength to stay patient. So we may sell our shares and watch as a powerful trend leaves us behind. Then we chase the breakout at high risk because our weak emotional state means that we lack patience and discipline. As soon as we enter at a high price the stock reverses and we are out with a large loss. Our emotional state continues to deteriorate and we continue to chase trying to make up our losses. The result is more losses. This is a self-destruct process that we must avoid.

For these reasons, we must pursue other interests besides trading. I don't mean we should take trading lightly. Trading is a serious endeavor that will challenge our mental, physical, and intellectual reserves. But being a serious trader does not require us to obsess over every price tick. Quite the opposite. Proper trading involves a lot of letting go and, quite frankly, not caring at a certain point. Letting go after entering a trade and putting in our stop order. Remember that the small rectangle within which Genworth's stock bounced around represents three weeks of our life. How stupid, wasteful, and weakening is it to worry about what a stock will do? If the stock moves higher, then fine. If the pattern fails, then our loss is limited to just a fraction of our trading account and we can look forward to other opportunities.

Lions Gate Entertainment: 5-month symmetrical triangle

Trading demands patience in many ways. We wait patiently for a breakout. We wait patiently for a resolution after a breakout. Patience also means persistent diligence in following a chart for weeks and months and even years as the price action evolves. The next chart shows the importance of not quitting on a chart after a decisive breakout stalls.

Let's look at the weekly chart to get an overall sense of the pattern:

FIGURE 35

It is a classical pattern as elegant, well-formed, and simple as the very first chart we looked at. But trading is also about the details, specifically, advantageous entries and loss-limiting exits. And upon closer examination, we had to meet successfully a couple of stiff challenges to trade this set-up well.

The next chart is a daily chart that focuses on the breakout and the subsequent price action:

FIGURE 35.1

The breakout from the 5-month symmetrical triangle, shown on the left part of the daily chart, was decisive. The stock rose in the following week but soon stalled and it looked as if there may be a hard retest of the upper boundary when prices declined in late September. But there was no hard retest and prices made steady gains over the next month. Two months have now passed since the breakout. The quarterly earnings report was due soon. Prices declined sharply in the week leading up to the earnings release. Then prices jumped 14% on earnings news but there was still no resolution to the fact that the stock had been essentially trading in the 14.50 to 16.50 range since the breakout. Indeed, the stock remained in this range for another two months.

It would have been understandable to quit on this pattern and move on to other set-ups. And we should look at set-ups where a breakout may be imminent. But there is also much value to continuing to keep up with "old" patterns because a relatively small but powerful pattern can develop over several weeks. Realize the effectiveness of a brief but focused look at a pattern every couple of days or so. Here, such continuous diligence allowed us to spot a smaller symmetrical triangle develop. The breakout came on a gap up in price. We could have entered around the closing price of the breakout day and set our stop somewhere below the upper boundary and remain well below our maximum risk. The stock marched higher from here.

So in a sense this second smaller triangle launched the "real" uptrend. There was no way to anticipate this development other than to stay patient and continue to monitor the chart.

Lincoln National Corp.: 15-month reversal symmetrical triangle

This symmetrical triangle was a reversal pattern. Here's the weekly chart:

FIGURE 36

Next is the daily chart with a focus on the breakout and retest:

FIGURE 36.1

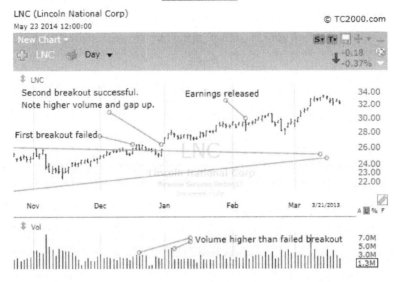

The first breakout failed when prices closed decisively below the upper boundary within a week. Failed breakouts, disappointing and jarring as they may be, do not necessarily mean that the pattern has also failed. We will find that some breakouts succeed only on their second or even third attempt. But we do need to move on at some point. I will consider trading a second breakout attempt but will almost always move on after the second try.

Here, the second breakout was successful. The higher volume and gap up in price strongly supported the view that this second breakout was the real breakout. What isn't so clear is whether we should trade this breakout. The gap up meant that we would have to chase this breakout to enter the trade. It wasn't unreasonable to chase if we bought a smaller position. Or we could have let this breakout go on its way without us. There will always be other opportunities, including set-ups where we don't have to chase at all.

Lastly, note that the day before the second breakout, the stock closed modestly but clearly above the upper boundary of the symmetrical triangle. I think that this re-close above the boundary offered a good chance to buy shares and set our stop just below the retest low. The possible downside was defined and limited while the upside was potentially much greater, which is a concise and cogent definition of good trading.

Cheniere Energy: 7-month symmetrical triangle

The next example involves another tricky breakout. The following weekly chart shows a textbook symmetrical triangle that formed from May to November 2013:

<u>FIGURE 37</u>

Weekly charts are useful because they give us perspective and a sense of the overall situation. But they can hide the gritty details of a breakout, and the particularities of every set-up can reveal both obstacles that we need to deal with or avoid as well as edges that we can take advantage of.

The next chart, a daily chart, reveals a tricky breakout:

FIGURE 37.1

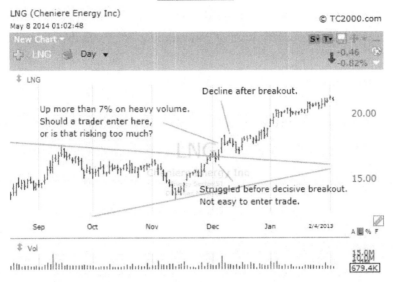

The stock closed above the upper boundary of the symmetrical triangle on the last trading day in November. While not a decisive breakout, buying shares here with a stop just below the low of the day was a reasonable entry with limited risk. The next day the stock traded a bit below the upper boundary but closed above it. A more severe retest came the following day as the stock closed below the upper boundary and also triggered any stop set just below the breakout day's low. Anything is possible at any point on a chart. The stock could continue to decline and the pattern could fail before evolving into a completely different set-up. Or it could attempt another breakout. I think the best thing to do in this situation, if we were stopped out, is to simply wait and see how the chart develops. We didn't have to wait long as the stock closed above the upper boundary the next day. Should we buy shares again here? Some of us, as a matter of principle, may decide to never trade more than once the same set-up. The pattern works the first time or does not.

If we are still interested in trading this pattern, what factors should we consider? The first factor is, as always, risk management. Does the set-up offer an advantageous entry spot? Here, the answer was yes. We could buy shares when the stock re-closed above the pattern boundary and set our stop just below the lowest reach of the hard retest. Our risk was well-defined and likely very limited. If we got stopped out again, then we could move on.

Volume was another factor to consider. The next chart focuses on the price action and volume in the breakout area:

FIGURE 37.2

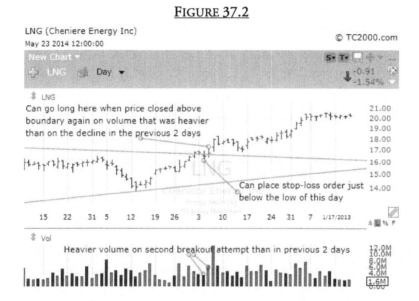

The volume on the hard retest was lower than during the initial breakout and the second breakout after the hard retest. It was possible to interpret this volume action as hinting that there was greater enthusiasm and strength among buyers than sellers. But this was just one possible interpretation. It was not and could never be a certainty.

Another factor to consider was that although the stock re-closed above the upper boundary, it did so by a small margin.

So we had to weigh the volume action, which seemed to favor the upside, against a hesitant breakout, which made another hard retest very possible.

I would re-enter this trade around the closing price of the second breakout based on the favorable volume action and, most importantly, the fact that my potential loss was very limited while the upside was much greater. In this case, I would have been rewarded with a 7% price jump on heavy volume the next day. But we're far from being done with this chart.

Next question: is it too late to enter this trade after the 7% jump? We know that powerful breakouts can make entering trades difficult by forcing us to chase and risk more than we would like. The situation is sometimes so difficult and risky that not trading the breakout is the correct decision. But we need not rule out chasing if we can chase while staying under our maximum risk. Here, buying a position that was about one-third to one-half the size of our normal position made our risk acceptable even if we placed our stop below the low of the hard retest.

And I think setting our stop down there was better than placing it, say, just below the low of the day when the stock increased 7%. While the 7% increase on heavy volume seemed to confirm the pattern and breakout, there was no guarantee that the stock would only go up from here. Indeed, the stock reversed immediately after the 7% jump and declined over the next week.

While this decline did not reach the pattern boundary, it would have triggered a stop set just below the low of the 7% day. The stock lost all of its 7% gain and then some. And the stock could decline farther and still stay above the upper boundary. Prices could return all the way back to the upper boundary before reversing and launching a powerful uptrend.

So a reasonable spot to place our stop-loss order is below either the low of the hard retest or the low of the day before the 7% jump. While we could place a stop at a higher price, it meant an increased chance that our position will get stopped out. Getting stopped out for a small loss is not the problem. The danger in this situation is getting caught in a painful and destructive downward spiral. We'll discuss this risk next.

Yoda said something about anger and suffering

We can get caught in a negative spiral if we get angry, frustrated, and greedy after we get stopped out by the price decline following the 7% jump. If we simply accept our small loss and move on, then there is no problem. But there is a problem if we get obsessed with making money from this pattern and we rashly buy shares again. Then we set our stop very close to our entry because we want to keep this emotional trade on a short leash and we cannot bear the thought of losing more money. But normal volatility stops us out again. We get angry and buy another position. And so on. Our losses pile up. The situation become very dangerous if we decide to simply not place a stop-loss order because we believe the pattern "has to work." A big loss results if we refuse to get out even as the stock continues to fall. The ultimate danger is if we convince ourselves that the pattern, despite these early difficulties, will work given its textbook shape and therefore go all in.

What led us to this self-destruction? Greed and fear. We wanted to make a lot of money right now with this pattern. We feared moving on could mean never finding another good set-up. As ridiculous as this fear may look to us as readers, we are all susceptible to such short-sightedness when we are fearful and angry.

Contrast this painful experience against traders who are unattached to the outcome of any single trade. Let's say some traders chase the breakout with a smaller-than-usual position and set their stop just below the low of the hard retest. If they get stopped out, then they are not bothered much about losing a small fraction of their trading account. They know that they have given this trade a fair chance to work. They move on to other opportunities. They may not even check back until weeks or even months later as they are busy doing other things. Had they followed every price move, they would have been strongly tempted to sell their position after the stock erased all of its gains from the 7% jump.

Finally, note how things were far from easy even if we had bought shares the day before the 7% jump. We were soon sitting on a 7% profit, but this profit cushion did not make weathering the ensuing price decline easy if we were anxiously watching the price action. All of us are susceptible to fear and frustration if we watch our profits get chipped away day after day. We need to let go after entering a trade.

Unfortunately, every trader is likely to experience this negative spiral. And we are most likely to fall into this diabolical trap when we forget that there will always be more profitable set-ups. A good way to recover our composure is to open this book and see how many intriguing patterns have appeared in U.S. stocks in just the past couple of years.

We should do this now: grab pen and paper and write "THERE WILL ALWAYS BE MORE GREAT SET-UPS" and post it on the wall. Say and believe these words every day.

Northrop Grumman: 5-month symmetrical triangle

The next chart shows the situation in Northrop Grumman from August 2012 to March 2013:

FIGURE 38

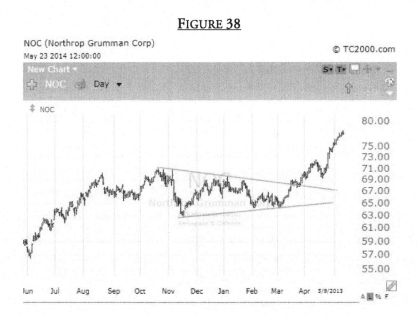

Northrop Grumman made strong gains up to August 2012 then stalled and traded between $65 and 70 for eight months. The second half of this range-bound price action turned into a symmetrical triangle that launched another strong uptrend.

The next chart focuses on the breakout:

FIGURE 38.1

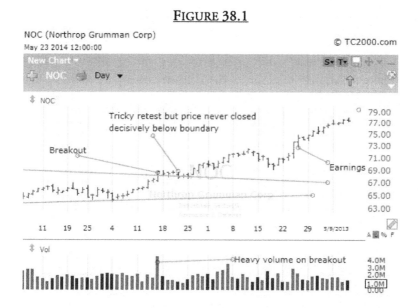

Heavy volume accompanied the decisive breakout through the upper boundary of the symmetrical triangle. If we had bought shares around the close of the breakout day and set a stop just below the low, we would risk about 2% of our position on a pattern that held much promise give its size, shape, and breakout. But, as always, these positive factors did not mean that the pattern was guaranteed to work.

Indeed, prices hugged the upper boundary for more than a week after breaking out. Four days after the breakout, prices closed slightly below the boundary. Prices continued to trade just above and below the upper boundary for two more days before breaking out of this congestion that included four hard retests. If we were checking the price action often, then we were much more likely to lose our discipline and sell our shares. Then, of course, we would have missed the upward surge that started just days later.

Again: enter and forget. Repeat.

Lastly, note how the hard retests didn't get close to triggering a stop placed just below the low of the breakout day.

<u>Principal Financial: 9-month symmetrical triangle</u>

The next chart includes an early look at a very interesting and useful pattern, a H&S top *failure* pattern. I learned this pattern from Peter L. Brandt. We will look at many more H&S top failure patterns in Chapter 16. These patterns are H&S tops that start an upward price move when prices decisively close above the high of the right shoulder.

Figure 39 is a weekly chart that gives us the big-picture view of the set-up:

FIGURE 39

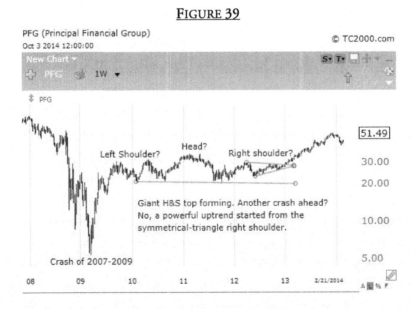

This stock had traded above $50 in 2008 before losing 90% of its value during the global financial crisis of 2007 to 2009. The stock recovered rapidly from the lows of spring 2009 as it increased five-fold in six months. Then it traded between $20 and $30 for 3 years. By the middle of 2012, the stock seemed to be forming a giant H&S top. The left shoulder, head, and possible right shoulder of this potential H&S top were clearly visible by the middle of 2012. Note how the possible right shoulder formed a symmetrical triangle. If this massive 3-year topping pattern was going to become a H&S top, then we would look for the stock to break down from this symmetrical-triangle right shoulder.

The next chart is a daily chart that focuses on the symmetrical-triangle right shoulder and the breakout:

FIGURE 39.1

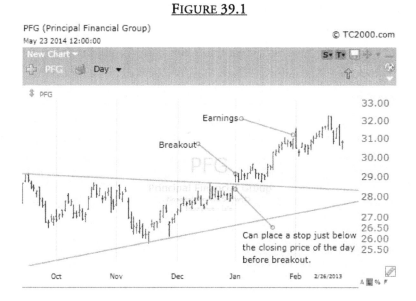

Instead of breaking down through the lower boundary of the symmetrical triangle, the stock gapped up through the upper boundary. The stock went on to gain more than 50% in the following year.

We didn't have to interpret this multi-year set-up as an H&S top failure. We could have looked at the set-up as a textbook 8-month symmetrical triangle that formed after a multi-year trading range.

But I have two reasons for discussing this set-up as a H&S top failure.

First, as we will discuss in Chapter 16, this pattern can be very useful and powerful. The more patterns and thus more possibilities we know, the more productive and creative we can be.

Second, the possible H&S top would have been a massive topping pattern had it been completed. The fact that a pattern this big failed suggested that the new trend could be similarly massive. Some of the most powerful trends start when a stock goes in the opposite direction from the expected direction. That said, some of us will prefer to look at this set-up as simply a symmetrical triangle. After all, the triangle was a large pattern on its own that could start a powerful move. Whatever our preferred interpretation, our goal is to continuously acquire knowledge, including different perspectives, to gain as much an edge as possible. A little edge can make a big difference.

In terms of trading tactics, we could buy shares around the closing price of the breakout day and place a stop just below the closing price of the day before rather than just below the low of the breakout day. In this case, we have to modify the last day rule for placing stops because the breakout day did not have any trading inside the pattern boundary due to the gap up in price. We could place our stop a bit lower or even below the low of the day before. Our stop placement depends on our trading style and risk tolerance. The most important thing is that we stay below our maximum risk in every trade.

Parker Drilling: 2-month symmetrical triangle

Our next symmetrical triangle was another instance where volume helped us analyze the situation:

FIGURE 40

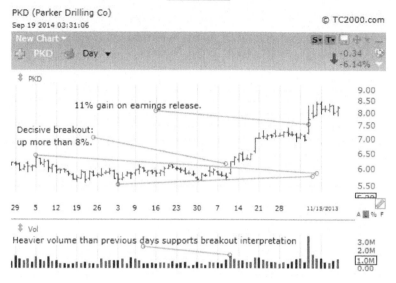

Volume helped us in two ways.

First, the volume generally declined as the symmetrical triangle formed. One of the requirements of a textbook symmetrical triangle is decreasing volume during pattern formation. That said, I feel that declining volume is not an absolute requirement and I have seen many symmetrical triangles that work well without a clear trend of declining volume. But when there is volume confirmation, then it can be an important factor supporting the pattern interpretation.

Second, the fact the breakout occurred on volume that was heavier than any day during pattern formation strongly suggested that the pattern boundary and the breakout through it had significance. In fact, the breakout day's heavy volume was not exceeded until a month later when extremely heavy volume accompanied the earnings report.

The breakout came on an 8% price jump. As we have seen, a decisive breakout can be both exciting and daunting. The 8% surge made the breakout decisive but the trade riskier. If I were to trade this breakout, I would buy a position that was about one half of my normal position size at around the breakout day's closing price and set my stop just below the breakout day's low. This trade would gain about 15% in two weeks. Then I would sell my shares before the earnings release. If I were to gamble on earnings, then I would keep at most one-third of my original position knowing that the stock could drop by double digits in response to the earnings report. Had I stayed in, I got lucky as the market's positive reaction to the earnings report sent the stock higher by almost 20% in the next three days. But remember that getting lucky is not the same thing as trading well by doing the right thing. While nothing guarantees a profit in a trade, doing the right thing over many trades is the best strategy for long-term profitability.

Rite Aid Corp.: 7-week symmetrical triangle

Our next symmetrical triangle formed in Rite Aid after the stock had gone up more than 50% in two months:

FIGURE 41

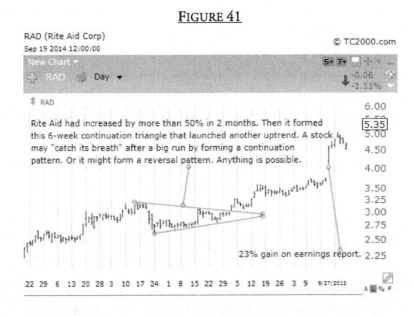

The breakout came on a decisive 4.3% gap up. The next day the stock went up another 4.5%. But not many breakouts go straight in the anticipated direction. Here, the stock declined 5% over the next three days. And the stock still had more room to decline before touching the upper boundary in what would be a normal retest. So, again, few things are as easy as they look. The only thing we can do is to enter a trade, set a stop, and move on.

Let's talk about trading this set-up.

First, the forceful breakout made buying shares and setting our stop a bit tricky. Buying shares around the closing price of the breakout day and setting our stop reasonably far away meant risking about 4.5% to 5% of our position. Depending on our maximum risk and trading style, we may decide to buy a smaller position than usual. Let's say we decide to be cautious, which is always a good approach, and buy a position that is about half the size of our normal position size.

Second, where could we place our stop? Notice that we need to modify the last day rule for placing a stop because the gap up meant that there was no trading within the pattern during the breakout day. Some possible places for our stop orders are: (1) just under the pattern's upper boundary, (2) just under the closing price of the day before breakout, or (3) just under the low price of the day before breakout.

A hard retest was likely to trigger a stop placed just below the upper boundary and even a stop placed below the closing price of the day before. Simply lowering our stop placement was not so easy to do because doing so meant risking even a larger portion of our already reduced position.

This set-up is a great example of how a textbook pattern and a decisive breakout are not necessarily the best trades. Trading is all about advantageous entries and loss-limiting stops. We must not trade just because there is a breakout. Knowing when not to trade is an important skill. The specifics of the Rite Aid set-up and breakout did not create the most favorable entry point and stop level. But the set-up wasn't so unfavorable as to call for automatic disqualification. We have options. First, we could pass. Second, we could buy a smaller position and set our stop somewhere below the upper boundary. And third, we could enter a position and place our stop somewhere above the upper boundary and hope that a hard retest does not occur. There is no right answer. If we decide to trade and choose either the second or third option, we must not get obsessed over making money on this pattern if we get stopped out. If I were stopped out, then I would move on without trying a second time because I know there will be many set-ups and breakouts with much more favorable entry and exit points.

NxStage Medical: 6-week reversal symmetrical triangle

Our next symmetrical triangle was a bottoming pattern that reversed a sharp downtrend. Volume helped us make sense of this pattern:

FIGURE 42

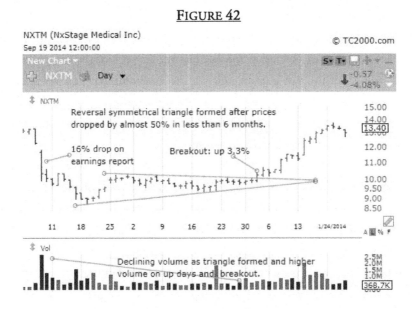

In a textbook bottoming reversal symmetrical triangle that launches an uptrend, the first major touch point would be with the line that would become the lower boundary, the second touch with the line that would become the upper boundary, the third touch with the lower boundary, the fourth touch again with the upper, and a fifth major contact with the lower boundary. Then the stock would break out through the upper boundary. In

Figure 42, we have four solid alternating touches with the lower and upper boundaries but we don't have the fifth touch on the lower boundary. But patterns don't have to be perfect to be useful and profitable. The stock was clearly coiling and forming a symmetrical triangle of some kind. Would this triangle continue the previous downtrend or reverse the downtrend and start a new uptrend?

Let's see if volume provided clues.

First, volume steadily declined as prices coiled into a triangle. This fact supported the interpretation that a meaningful coil was taking place.

Second, volume was higher on up days than on down days. This fact supported the interpretation that buyers were more enthusiastic than sellers and thus the bias could be to the upside, though we could never be sure. Note how volume spiked as the stock went from the first touch point on the lower boundary to the second touch point on the upper boundary. Volume then declined as the stock declined to the lower boundary. An even larger volume spike occurred as the stock went up from the third touch point to the fourth. Volume decreased again as the stock declined from the upper boundary. Note prices did not go all the way down to the lower boundary, which would have been the textbook fifth touch. Finally, volume increased as the stock broke through the upper boundary. A powerful uptrend followed.

So we should be mindful of the volume accompanying the price action without falling into the trap of thinking that it is infallible.

Some cautionary points.

The chart does not fully capture the volatile nature of this stock. Large daily price moves were common. We're happy when we're on the same side of a powerful trend. But we have to remember that sharp trends can reverse quickly. We have to bring to every trade the utmost caution and prudence: enter a trade only when the reward-to-risk ratio is favorable, always use stops that limit losses, and take at least some profits at measured priced targets.

Also, it was easy to miss the breakout from this relatively small 6-week pattern. If we missed the breakout, then we must not chase and exceed our risk parameters. It is frustrating to watch a powerful trend take off without us. When such frustration hits, our job is to remember that there will always be more opportunities.

CHAPTER 12

Continuation Pennant (Small Triangle)

Pennants are small triangles that sometimes form after a powerful run or soon after a breakout. We can think of them as when stocks take a breather before starting another run.

Capella Education

Figure 43 is a weekly chart that shows a 9-month reversal symmetrical triangle that formed from July 2012 to April 2013:

FIGURE 43

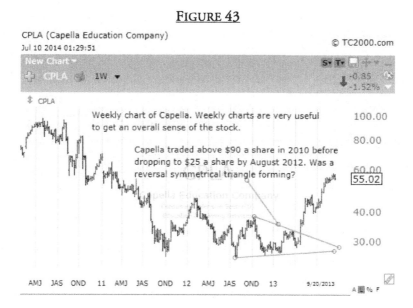

CPLA (Capella Education Company)
Jul 10 2014 01:29:51   © TC2000.com

New Chart ▾   S▾ T▾ ☐ ◈ ▾
✛ CPLA 🔔 1W ▾   ▼ -0.85 ⚙
                                                            -1.52%

$ CPLA

Weekly chart of Capella. Weekly charts are very useful   100.00
to get an overall sense of the stock.
                                                            80.00
Capella traded above $90 a share in 2010 before
dropping to $25 a share by August 2012. Was a
reversal symmetrical triangle forming?   60.00
                                                         [55.02]

                                                            40.00

                                                            30.00

AMJ JAS OND 11 AMJ JAS OND 12 AMJ JAS OND 13   9/20/2013   A ▣ % F

And the following chart, Figure 43.1, is a daily chart that focuses on the reversal triangle in the bottom right portion of Figure 43:

FIGURE 43.1

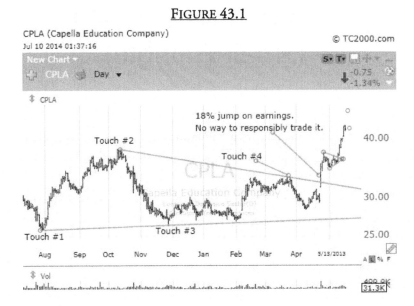

Some of us may object that this price action is not a reversal symmetrical triangle. There is something about it that is ungainly. We might also note that it has only four touch points compared to the five touch points of a textbook reversal symmetrical triangle. These are valid objections. And there is nothing wrong with moving on to other charts if we don't believe in the pattern or see anything interesting. We have to believe in and be excited about the pattern's possibilities to trade the pattern well using good risk management. If we don't see a valid reversal symmetrical triangle, then how can we trade it?

Let's stay on this point. I am always amazed at how often I look at another trader's "H&S top" or a "descending triangle" and I don't see these patterns. Sometimes I see the pattern but they are too loosely formed for my preference. Remember that it is a good idea to try to trade only patterns that can be used as textbook examples. Other times I just don't see any price action resembling the named pattern. We must not trade a chart just because another trader says there is a pattern. The temptation to trade another trader's identified pattern will be strong if this trader is an "expert" who appears in the media. Some well-known traders do offer interesting analyses and insights, but in my experience only a very small portion of the charting analysis in the media has value.

Why might this be the case?

First, as mentioned, we many simply not see, for example, the H&S top that another trader has identified. Such disagreement results from the fact that traders may have different requirements for classical patterns. There is room for different opinions when interpreting charts. That said, we should try to stick as close as possible to Edwards & Magee's descriptions of each of the classical patterns. Edwards & Magee's classic text has proven to be timeless. We should not deviate too much from the fundamental principles that they have laid out.

Second, even if we agree with another trader that a H&S top may be forming, we are almost certain to have different entry and exit strategies and also different risk tolerances. In short, we have to do our own homework and stay within our comfort zone. Don't worry about what others are doing. Nobody has the single correct method. We need to focus on doing the right things, namely, entering at advantageous spots and limiting losses. How we accomplish these tasks is up to us. Classical charting offers traders different ways to trade the same pattern. And we should welcome the freedom, flexibility, and choice.

Let's return to the Capella chart. I would not have identified this chart as a reversal symmetrical triangle until the 18% jump in response to the earnings report. And of course it was impossible to anticipate this 18% gap up. Further, it was too risky to buy shares immediately after the breakout because we had to risk too much of our position to do so. So does this set-up have any value to us?

I think there are two takeaways.

First, we should be open minded. This reversal symmetrical triangle did not have the textbook-specified five major touches with the pattern boundaries and looked a bit "off" to some of us. But patterns don't have to be perfect to be useful. Remember how the reversal symmetrical triangle in Figure 42 did not have the fifth contact but still served as a useful and tradable interpretation of the price action.

Second, while we could not anticipate nor trade the 18% jump, the magnitude of this price gap suggested the possibility of a powerful trend to come. This big move arguably constituted the decisive breakout from a reversal symmetrical triangle. And while the breakout was untradeable, the stock could form another pattern, like a small continuation pattern, that might offer a compelling trading opportunity. So far we have not committed our money and are simply appraising different possibilities that may alert us to a trading opportunity. There was value to continuing to watch this chart. And we were rewarded with an opportunity to enter this trade through a continuation pennant that formed within 3 weeks of the 18% jump.

The next chart focuses on the price action following the untradeable breakout:

FIGURE 43.2

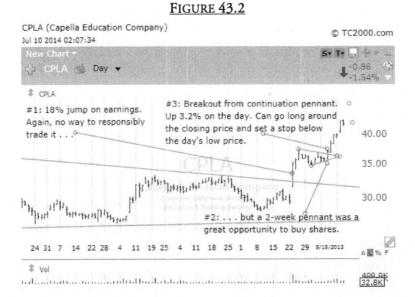

On the right side of the chart, we see a textbook continuation pennant (or, if you prefer, a small triangle) forming within a few weeks of the 18% breakout.

Small continuation patterns can be another and perhaps better opportunity to enter a trade if we missed the initial breakout or if the initial breakout was not tradable as in Capella. Small patterns like this pennant can start big moves. Here, prices increased 20% over the next week.

There would be another opportunity to buy shares, but not before our patience was tested. Before we discuss yet another entry opportunity, let's first note the volume bars. Capella is a volatile and thinly-traded stock. We must use extra caution when trading such stocks. The next chart focuses on the price action after prices broke out from the first pennant:

FIGURE 43.3

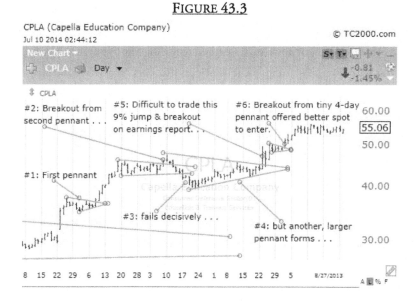

The first pennant produced a 20% gain in a week. Then prices paused and traded in a narrow range for the next three weeks. In fact, prices seemed to be coiling to form yet another continuation pennant. There seemed to be a decisive breakout from this second continuation pennant but, the next day, the breakout lost momentum and prices closed decisively below the upper boundary of this second pennant two days later. Prices continued to decline and plunged well below even the lower boundary of this failed pennant.

This second pennant failed decisively. But we had good reason to trade the breakout from the second pennant. This trade would have been based on a clear breakout from a well-shaped classical chart pattern. Remember that a good trade is not the same thing as a profitable trade. Buying shares after a clean breakout from the second pennant was a good trade even if the trade resulted in a loss because the trade had a favorable reward-to-risk possibility. We were justifiably, but not overly, disappointed when the pennant failed but we could confidently move on knowing that we limited our losses to just a small fraction of our trading capital.

Almost as important as limiting our loss is continuing to watch the chart. Continued attention did not require hourly or even daily looks at the chart. A focused glance every couple of days was enough to alert us to the possible development of another bigger continuation pennant. Prices broke out of this larger pennant when prices jumped 9% on earnings news. Incidentally, note that it was possible to interpret the price action from the failed second pennant to the breakout from the larger pennant as a continuation H&S bottom with a down-sloping neckline. But how we label a price action is of little importance compared to the utmost importance of managing our risk on every trade, and here, it was difficult to buy shares after a 9% jump that required us to risk up to 10% of our position.

As we should not hold a position through the earnings release, we should not have bought Capella shares in anticipation of a positive reaction to the earnings news. And by doing the right thing, we correctly "missed" the 9% gain. Should we buy shares towards the end of the breakout day? I say no because we were **out of position**. If we were to buy a regular position around the closing price of the breakout day and set our stop using the last day rule, then we would be risking almost 10% of our position. I think 10% is too much to risk no matter how exciting the set-up and breakout. We have to remember that the breakout from the second pennant failed only 6 weeks ago. And this breakout, too, could reverse and lead to pattern failure. The problem is not failed patterns. The problem is the excessive risk I would be taking on if I were to enter the trade after the breakout. Buying a smaller position is always an effective way to reduce risk.

The set-up tested our resolve and psyche even if we used a smaller position as there was hard retest of the upper boundary the very next day. Again, placing our stop reasonably far away, ideally below the low of the breakout day, was important. If we tried to get away with a stop placed closer to the upper boundary to lose less money if we were stopped out, then we got stopped out and faced a difficult situation. Do we enter again and risk getting stopped out again? I think it is important that if we decide to enter this trade after the breakout, we should do it right the first time: use a smaller position and set a wide enough stop to give our position a fair chance to survive normal volatility and even hard retests. If we get stopped out, we can move on knowing that we gave the trade a fair chance to work while staying below our risk limit.

Of course there was another option: do not trade the breakout, even with a smaller position. We don't have to trade every breakout. As we saw, some breakouts are untradeable. Much effort and discipline will be required to stop ourselves from chasing untradeable breakouts, especially if the stock is soaring and we are left behind. While this breakout from the larger pennant was not completely untradeable, it also was not the most favorable set-up. Even if we decided to stay out, we could continue to observe the chart. Several days later we saw prices trading in a very narrow range and making a very tight coil. Could another continuation pennant, this time a very small one, be forming? This development stresses the importance of diligently going through our charts. Simply checking in every couple of days would have alerted us to this 4-day pennant.

Since breakouts from pennants can be explosive, one way to trade a potential breakout from this possible pennant was to enter a buy stop order just above the preliminary upper boundary and set a sell stop order around just below the preliminary lower boundary. We would risk just over 3% of our position to possibly catch early a powerful breakout from this pennant.

Prices jumped 4.6% to decisively break out from the third pennant in three months.

If we did not want to use a buy-stop order and deal with its associated risks, then we were still in a good position to buy shares after the breakout. Buying shares around the closing price of the breakout day meant risking about 4.6% of our position, which is much less than the 9% we had to risk to chase the breakout from the large pennant. It always pays to continuously follow a chart's evolution.

CHAPTER 13
Ascending Wedge

The ascending or rising wedge is our next classical pattern. It has two rising boundaries lines where the lower boundary's angle of ascent is steeper than the upper boundary's slope. Despite its name, an ascending wedge is a bearish pattern that indicates a likely downtrend as prices break down through the lower boundary.

<u>PFL Energia: 10-week ascending wedge</u>

Our first ascending wedge is from PFL Energia, a Brazilian electric utility:

FIGURE 44

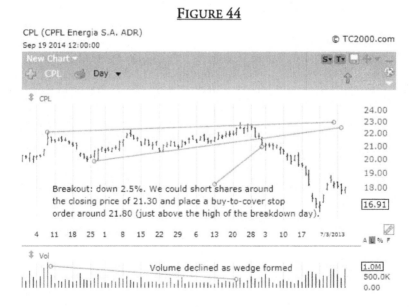

Note the generally declining volume during the formation of the wedge. As we noted, volume confirmation is not necessary but helpful when analyzing a pattern. Notice how the stock traded and even closed above the upper boundary of the wedge. Such peeking is common in rising wedges. The signal to go short came when prices closed decisively below the lower boundary. We could set our stop just above the high of the breakdown day. Finally, note the higher volume as the stock started to break down, which supported the downtrend interpretation. Everything about this rising wedge was by the book. Our bottom line will be much better if we strive to trade only such textbook set-ups.

Oriental Financial Group: 3-month ascending wedge

Our next ascending wedge is another textbook pattern. Figure 45 shows the overall set-up leading up to the formation of the wedge:

FIGURE 45

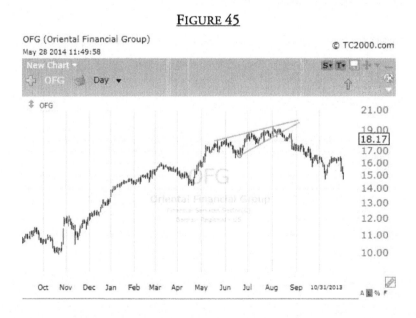

Oriental Financial's stock had doubled in price in 10 months and then started to form this ascending wedge. Remember, a reversal pattern needs something to reverse. The next chart focuses on the breakout area:

FIGURE 45.1

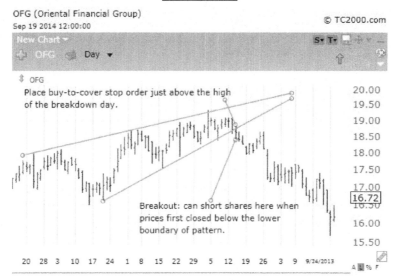

There was a retest of sorts as prices recovered a bit after breaking down through the lower boundary. But this semi-retest did not come close to challenging a stop placed above the high of the breakdown day.

The rising wedges that formed in CPFL Energia and Oriental Financial were truly textbook examples. But not all ascending wedges will be so elegant and clean. The most difficult aspect of trading rising wedges is similar to other patterns with slanting boundaries like symmetrical triangles and H&S patterns with slanting necklines: dealing with retests on a sloping boundary. A normal retest in a rising wedge could keep prices below the lower boundary yet still go higher than the breakout point. Such a retest can also trigger our stop-loss order and still stay under the wedge's lower boundary. The next chart shows how a possible retest could stay under the lower boundary while prices shot higher:

FIGURE 45.2

I can think of three ways to deal with such retests.

First, we simply move on when we are stopped out. If the rising wedge will not break down cleanly, then we are not interested in trading the pattern again.

Second, we can attempt one more trade if the stock closes just under the lower boundary after stopping us out. If the stock continues higher and stops us out for the second time, then we move on.

The third option is a somewhat drastic but not unreasonable choice: avoid trading rising wedges. After all, there are plenty of textbook patterns with horizontal or nearly horizontal boundaries. It is fine to trade, say, only rectangles and H&S set-ups. While I would not categorically eliminate patterns with slanting boundaries, I think **being selective in general is very good**. We must find our likings and strengths and stick to then and don't worry about what others are doing.

CHAPTER 14
Descending Wedge

Our next classical chart pattern is the descending or falling wedge. A descending wedge has two descending boundaries, with the upper boundary declining more steeply than the lower boundary. It is a bullish pattern that indicates the stock will likely rise after breaking out through the upper boundary.

Owens Illinois: 6-week descending wedge

Our first descending wedge is from the chart of Owens Illinois. Let's first get an overall view of the set-up:

FIGURE 46

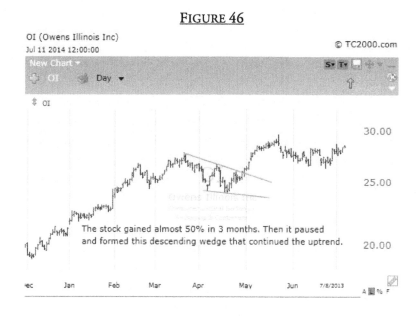

The stock rose almost 50% from December 2012 to March 2013. Then it paused and traded in the $24 to $28 range for the next 6 weeks. While a descending wedge is drawn on the chart, it was not so clear in mid-April whether a descending wedge was the most useful way to interpret the price action. The more obvious interpretation seemed to be a larger H&S top forming from February to April 2013:

FIGURE 46.1

It was not just the price action strongly suggesting a possible H&S top. It was not easy to believe that the stock would continue to rise after gaining almost 50% in such a short period. It was easier to believe that the strong uptrend was coming to an end that this possible H&S top would reverse the uptrend. On the other hand, it was also reasonable to interpret the price action from mid-March to mid-April as a bullish descending wedge.

What now?

As classical chartists, **we should not try to predict the future**. Instead, we should strive to **participate in trends launched by classical patterns**. So the best thing to do was to continue to observe the chart's evolution.

The next chart shows one way to trade the price action:

FIGURE 46.2

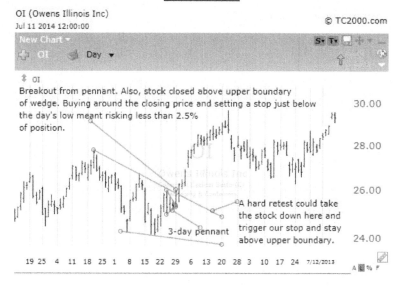

OI (Owens Illinois Inc)
Jul 11 2014 12:00:00

© TC2000.com

New Chart ▾

➕ OI 🌢 Day ▾

⬍ OI

Breakout from pennant. Also, stock closed above upper boundary
of wedge. Buying around the closing price and setting a stop just below
the day's low meant risking less than 2.5%
of position.

30.00

28.00

26.00

A hard retest could take
the stock down here and
3-day pennant   trigger our stop and stay
above upper boundary.   24.00

19 25   4   11   18   25   1   8   15   22   29   6   13   20   28   3   10   17   24   7/12/2013

If someone asked me what I thought about the price action in Owens
Illinois from February to April 2013, I would have said that it seemed like a
H&S top was forming. But my opinion was just that: an opinion. And
other traders had different opinions. Some of us may have preferred the
descending wedge interpretation. Whatever our view of the chart, there was
no reason to take a position unless there was a breakout from the H&S top
or the descending wedge. So while it is fine to have an opinion, we must
not be so committed and obsessed with a particular view as to blind
ourselves from the actual price action. We have to remain mentally nimble
despite our biases. The best way to remain flexible is to believe what we see
and not what we want to believe. This is easier said than done.

If we were so committed to the H&S top interpretation, then we would
not have seen a small pennant develop within the descending wedge. We
also would have missed a strong breakout to the upside from this pennant
that resulted in prices closing above the upper boundary of the descending
wedge. Don't get me wrong: there was no guarantee that this pennant and
descending wedge would work as the possible breakout could reverse at any

moment and the chart evolve into something completely different. But keeping an open mind would have at least alerted us to a possibly compelling entry opportunity.

On the other hand, if we were single-mindedly focused on a bullish descending wedge interpretation, then we were blind to a potentially powerful H&S top. If the upside breakout from the wedge reversed and failed, yet we had convinced ourselves that the wedge pattern "had to work," then we were vulnerable to taking risky and foolish actions, such as refusing to honor our stop or even adding to our losing position as the stock broke down through the neckline of the H&S top.

We might object that the 3-day pennant is too insignificant a development to trade on it. I sympathize with this objection, but I think it is also important to look for small edges. And trading well is about continuously exploiting small edges. The pennant need not carry some deep meaning. The breakout from the pennant, if we chose such an interpretation, was simply a chance to enter this trade on favorable terms. In exchange for risking 2.5% of our position, we could make far more if our interpretation worked. If the breakout from the pennant turned out to be nothing and we were stopped out soon, then we suffered a minor loss and we would move on.

Let's say that we either did not spot or think significant the breakout from the pennant and descending wedge. We wanted a more significant signal before going long or short. Was another trade setting up? Recall our brief description of the H&S top failure pattern above and then look at the next chart:

FIGURE 46.3

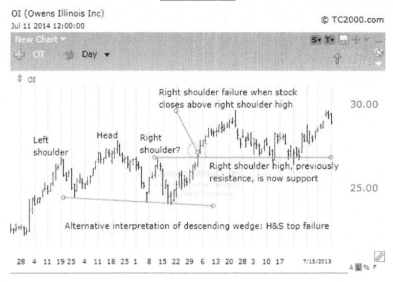

OI (Owens Illinois Inc)
Jul 11 2014 12:00:00
© TC2000.com

Figure 46.3 shows prices closing above what would have been the highest point of the right shoulder in a H&S top. This close signaled a completion of a H&S top failure pattern and was a chance to buy shares. The fact that the right-shoulder high later served as a support level confirmed that prices closing above the right shoulder was a meaningful event supporting the H&S top failure interpretation.

We may be overwhelmed by the multiple interpretations inherent in almost every chart. We might be frustrated at not seeing the alternative interpretations until too late. We must not worry. Time and experience will improve our ability to spot patterns and keep an open mind at the same time. We should take comfort in the versatility of chart patterns that allows for multiple interpretations and thus multiple entry points. Having more than one way to trade a set-up means that we often have another opportunity to enter a trade even if we missed the first breakout.

Parker Drilling: 10-week descending wedge

From February to April 2013, Parker Drilling formed the following textbook descending wedge:

FIGURE 47

While the wedge had textbook form, it required much patience in several ways to trade it well.

First, patience and discipline were required to stay out of this trade until the dust settled from the earnings release. The stock closed above the upper boundary of the wedge four days before the earnings release. It was tempting to enter the trade then and rationalize this entirely unpredictable gamble by thinking, "the stock must know that the earnings report will be good since it closed above the boundary just days before the earnings announcement." This is groundless and dangerous reasoning.

If the market reacts favorably to the earnings report and pushes prices up beyond our reach, then so be it. We move on to the many other set-ups that we can trade. If the market reacts negatively to earnings and crashes the price down through the upper and lower boundaries of the wedge, then we move on knowing that we did the right thing by staying out regardless of the market's reaction to earnings.

What is interesting is how often the market gives us enough time to enter a trade rather than putting the trade out of reach with an explosive move. Here, the day after the earnings announcement, the stock traded within the same narrow range as it did on earnings day. Also, with the immediate uncertainty of the earnings release out of the way, we had a logical entry and exit strategy. We could buy shares around the closing price of the day after the earnings release and set our stop at a reasonable distance away that still kept us well under our maximum risk. The rationale for this trade is that the earnings report did not cause prices to undo the breakout from the pattern. The breakout was still valid and we had an attractive entry point.

That said, the inherent trickiness in trading a pattern with slanting boundaries remained. While prices reacted calmly to the earnings report, prices could still retest the upper boundary and trigger our stop-loss order yet stay above the boundary. Given the inherent difficulty of trading a pattern with a slanting boundary, I would move on if stopped out and not attempt another trade.

Here, the stock jumped 9% two days after the earnings release. But the stock did everything but go straight up. Much patience was again required. The stock traded within the $4.20 and $4.90 range for the next six weeks. Six weeks of prices going sideways and nowhere. Only in hindsight is it easy to say holding patiently was the right thing to do for a big gain. We have heard it before and we must hear it again: it is impossible to stay patient and give a set-up time to work (or fail) unless we turn our attention to other charts and other interests. My general rule is that I try my very best to give a trade time to work itself out as long as my position is sitting on any kind of profit or is only slightly in the red.

Patience is perhaps the most important trait of a good trader. But, and there is always an exception, infinite patience may not be always appropriate. There will be other set-ups that never look back after breaking out. So another general rule I follow is that I may reduce my position size, say, to half of my original position, to free up capital for other trades if the stalling sideways price action continues for more than three weeks and a continuation pattern does not seem to be forming. If there are truly promising set-ups in other stocks, I may exit my entire position.

In Parker Drilling, the month-long sideways action following the early-May breakout would have tried my patience. The sharp decline into early June would be frustrating for many traders. But difficult moments often offer important clues. Notice how the early-June decline held above the $4.10 level and did not trade or close below our possible initial entry point. Prices staying above this crucial support level supported the view that the early-May breakout had continuing significance and that there were buyers when the stock returned to the breakout price. The stock started to surge a week after it successfully stayed above this level. If the stock failed to hold this support level, then not only would I have been stopped out but I would not have tried to trade this set-up again. I had given the pattern plenty of time to work and a crucial support level had failed. It would be time to move on.

Stifel Financial: 10-week descending wedge

Our last descending wedge combined a textbook shape with a tricky breakout:

FIGURE 48

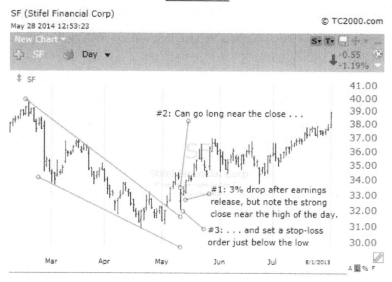

SF (Stifel Financial Corp)
May 28 2014 12:53:23

© TC2000.com

#2: Can go long near the close . . .

#1: 3% drop after earnings
release, but note the strong
close near the high of the day.

#3: . . . and set a stop-loss
order just below the low

Prices broke out of the descending wedge five days before the earnings release. Was it worth buying a position here? We certainly don't have to, but if we are looking for a quick trade, an entry here could be worthwhile because a stock may run up quite a bit in the days leading up to the earnings report. Prices increased by 5% in the four days between breakout and earnings. If we entered this quick trade, we should sell our shares before the earnings release.

It is always interesting to watch the stock's reaction to the earnings report. Sometimes a stock trades as if nothing happened by trading with less volatility than normal. Other times, a stock makes a huge gap up or gap down. And sometimes an earnings release will lead to great initial volatility that settles down and clarifies the picture. In Figure 48, the earnings report led to a gap down in price. However, the stock reversed the downward momentum by the end of the day. The stock was still down 3% for the day, but the momentum seemed to be to the upside as the stock closed near the high of the day. Had we gambled by staying in our position through earnings, it was likely that we got scared and sold near the low of the day or simply got stopped out for a loss. If we did not trade through earnings, and we should not have, then we now had the opportunity to enter on much more favorable terms and with the immediate volatility and utter unpredictability of the earnings report behind us. We could buy shares around the closing price of the day and place our stop-loss order just below the low.

Finally, note again the patience required to ride the big moves. The stock initially surged after the earnings-day reversal. Then it traded within the $34 and $37 range for the next month before breaking through.

CHAPTER 15
Flags and Channels

A descending flag looks like a down-sloping parallelogram. Flags that are anywhere from several days to three to four weeks in duration are similar to continuation pennants in that they are often form after big runs. Breakouts from flags often start another strong move that continues the previous trend.

Descending flags usually form after a strong move up and are usually down-slanting or horizontal and indicate the possible continuation of the uptrend. Ascending flags form after a decline and are usually up-slanting or straight and indicate the possible continuation of the downtrend.

Edwards & Magee specified that true flags should not form for more than 2-3 weeks. It has been my experience that small flags ranging from several days to two weeks are often the best trades. However, I have also found success with much larger flags, sometimes months in duration. Every classical pattern has countless variations. We can study the following charts, learn some of the many possibilities, and pick the trading style that we like. Which pattern we trade is far less important than that we trade each set-up using prudent risk management.

Clearwater Paper: 7-week descending flag

Our first flag launched a breakout from a yearlong rectangle. Figure 49 provides an overall view of the set-up:

FIGURE 49

The next chart focuses on the breakout:

FIGURE 49.1

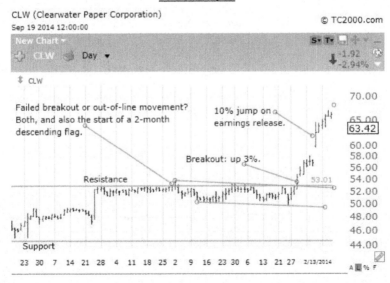

Note the failed breakout after prices traded just under the upper-boundary resistance level for a month. This failure suggested that there were many sellers at that level. So many, in fact, that gathering momentum for a month was not enough to break through resistance. Then the stock formed a down-slanting flag. One possible interpretation of the price action was that the stock was again gathering momentum to break through resistance. Here, a decisive breakout from the flag also led to a decisive breakout from the yearlong rectangle pattern.

There are several takeaways with this setup.

First, a small pattern within a larger pattern can initiate the overall breakout and start a big move.

Second, we must not underestimate old resistance and support levels. Resistance and support levels formed months, years, and even decades ago can have force today. Here, the March 2013 high served as powerful resistance almost a year later.

Third, breakouts sometimes succeed only after several attempts, especially when the breakout must surmount a longstanding resistance or support level. If we have been stopped out a couple of times due to failed breakouts, then we may be hesitant to try again. And it is perfectly fine to move on. There will be many set-ups that will break out cleanly on the first attempt. Here, there were six failed breakouts in the two months leading up to the real breakout. Prices traded above but failed to close decisively above the pattern boundary during these failed breakouts. The real breakout, in contrast, was unmistakable. So another lesson is to wait for the unmistakable breakout (which can still fail). The advantage of waiting is that the situation clarifies. While a powerful breakout can make entering the trade too risky, in my experience more often than not charts provide a favorable spot to enter even after a decisive breakout. And if it is too risky to chase, then we must have the discipline to move on.

Cts Corp.: 6-week descending flag

Our next flag formed after the stock gained 50% in three months. The following chart provides a big-picture view of the set-up:

FIGURE 50

Next, the close-up of the pattern and breakout:

FIGURE 50.1

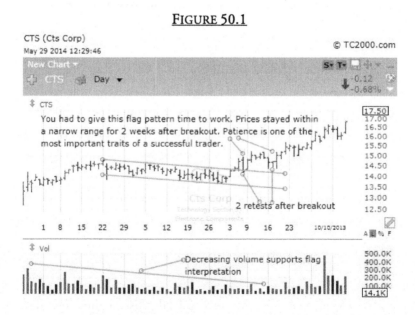

Let's first note that CTS often had very low daily-trading volume. I always use a smaller position with thinly-traded stocks like CTS. Also, the declining volume during the formation of the flag supported the pattern interpretation.

The breakout was decisive, but the follow-through was not. There were two retests in the next 10 days.

The first retest was a hard retest that came the day after breakout and led to the stock closing below the upper boundary. Prices did not close below the boundary by much but the hard retest would have triggered a stop-loss order placed just below the low of the breakout day given that the breakout day had very little trading within the pattern boundary. In such a case, it is prudent to set our stop farther away from the boundary.

The second retest came a week after the breakout. While it did not touch the upper boundary, it nonetheless would have been discouraging to a trader who was impatiently waiting for a strong uptrend and who was anxiously watching the price action. As always, the correct thing to do is to enter, set our stop, and turn our energy and attention elsewhere. Had we turned to other charts and projects and forgotten about this trade, then we would find that the stock had broken through the post-breakout congestion two weeks later and made large gains.

Patrick Industries: 10-week descending flag

Our next descending flag formed in another low-volume stock:

FIGURE 51

Some classical chartists may argue that this pattern is not a true flag because it is too long in duration. We noted that Edwards & Magee defined flags as rather small patterns that last no longer than two to three weeks. I still trade large "flags" because I think of them as variations to the standard small flag. More important than the pattern's label is whether we can find an advantageous entry point and logical stop-loss point. And I think this large descending flag provided a favorable trade set-up.

The next chart focuses on the breakout:

FIGURE 51.1

We could buy shares as soon as prices closed above the upper boundary or wait for a more decisive breakout, which came the next day. As Patrick Industries is another low-volume stock, we would use a smaller position to further limit risk. Using a smaller position allows us to set our stop at a reasonable distance from the upper boundary and still remain below our maximum risk.

Federated Investors: 3-month descending flag

Our next large descending flag is one of my favorites. Volume declined during pattern formation and increased during the breakout and the strong follow through:

FIGURE 52

Altisource Portfolio Solutions: 5-month descending flag

Our next flag might be called a giant descending flag:

FIGURE 53

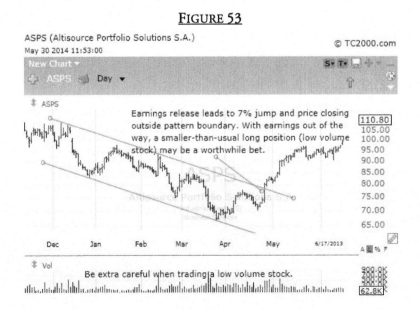

We have seen how quarterly earnings reports affect our trading. Here, the stock broke out and closed above the upper boundary on earnings news. With the immediate volatility caused by the earnings release behind us, we might consider buying shares around the closing price. Because the stock was up 7% on the breakout day, we would likely buy a smaller position to stay within our risk parameter. Another reason to buy a smaller position is the fact that Altisource Portfolio is a relatively volatile low-volume stock. We must always use extra caution when trading a thinly-traded stock. We may be tempted to use a large position or rashly go all-in with thin stocks because we think about how fast they can move and produce big profits. But fast-moving stocks don't always move in our favor. Fast moves go in both directions.

By the way, the giant flag is my own label. Edwards & Magee would likely identify Figure 53 as a descending channel. They wrote that the breaking of a channel line is not a trade signal as it may signal only a change in the technical situation rather than a definite change in the trend. They argued that traders should wait until a classical pattern forms after the breaking of a channel line. I agree mostly with Edwards & Magee's analysis and prescription. Channels by definition have slanting boundaries and thus are subject to all the additional difficulties associated with trading patterns with non-horizontal boundaries. Also, large channels, despite my labeling them "giant flags," reflect an entirely different price action compared to the compact flags that Edwards & Mage had in mind. Flags are relatively brief rest periods within a narrow trading range. They usually form after a stock has made a strong run. In contrast, channels, or giant flags, cover a much larger trading range and do not form after a strong run.

I will at least consider trading channel breaks because I have seen fast moves come from them. As long as I manage my risk and stay within my comfort zone on every trade, I am comfortable trading patterns in a way that the founders of classical charting may not have envisioned. It is fine for us to develop our own trading style that still follows most of the fundamental rules of classical charting. I consider trading giant flags as a relatively minor extension of classical charting principles. Classical charting offers us choices. As we learn and gain experience, we will develop our own trading style. We should take advantage of the fact that classical charting principles are flexible and allow for personalization.

While I am open to trading breakouts from channels, I would much prefer to trade breakouts from flags. I have found it more difficult to trade channel breakouts compared to flag breakouts. Thus, I move on if there is no immediate and decisive follow through after the breakout from the channel. Patience is vital in trading, but I give less leeway to certain set-ups. Channels are such instances.

Cray Inc.: 4-month descending flag

Here's another giant descending flag:

FIGURE 54

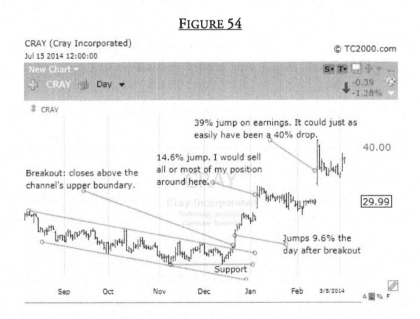

The breakout day from this 4-month channel in Cray Inc. was an ideal spot to buy shares. While the stock clearly closed above the channel's upper boundary, it did not do so by such a large margin as to make entering the trade too risky. Indeed, the stock was up a modest 1.1% on the breakout day and thus allowed us to risk no more than 2% of our position if we chose to buy shares around the closing price of the breakout day and set our stop just below the low price. It turned out that the breakout day was not just a good day but perhaps the last day to buy shares as the stock jumped almost 10% the next day.

Is it too late to buy shares after the 10% jump? I think reasonable minds can differ. Some will argue that the initial "breakout" was not decisive enough, that this 10% gain was the real breakout and the better trade signal. Others will argue that risking close to 12% of our position, even a reduced position, in a single trade is simply too much. I would have passed on this trade if I had not bought shares at the initial breakout. Again, reasonable minds will differ. If we decide to buy shares after the 10% jump, then we must significantly reduce our position size to stay under our maximum risk.

Cray made strong gains after the breakout, culminating in a 39% gain on earnings news. Before we say "see, that's why it's worth gambling on earnings releases," we have to remember that the large gain could just as easily have been a huge loss.

Olin Corp.: 7-month descending flag

As in Figure 54, our next descending giant flag pattern featured a modest but clear breakout followed by strong gains:

FIGURE 55

There was a retest a week after breakout but the retest did not threaten a stop placed below the breakout day's low.

Hilltop Holdings: 5-month descending flag

We have another textbook channel:

FIGURE 56

The breakout was very decisive – up almost 5% on the day. This strong gain meant that some of us, depending on our risk tolerance, would have bought a smaller position to trade the breakout. I would have used my regular position size because I thought the set-up and breakout were very promising. First, the upper boundary had clearly been acting as a strong resistance level as it rejected at least five attempts to break above it. Second, the breakout was decisive on volume that was much higher than on previous days. Third, because the earnings report led to the breakout, entering around the closing price of the day and after earnings had been released meant that we did not have to deal with the immediate volatility of earnings news. Lastly, the breakout from the channel also meant a breakout from a small H&S bottom within the channel. I am more confident, though never certain, about a trade when a smaller pattern launches a breakout from a larger pattern.

Buying shares around the closing price of the breakout day and placing a stop below the low price meant risking about 5% of our position. Five percent may be the upper limit of our maximum risk for a single trade. We may feel more comfortable buying a smaller-than-usual position. As I said, I give less leeway when trading channel breakouts. If they don't start working immediately, then I'm out and looking for other set-ups. Whether or not we decide to trade channel breakouts, we can benefit by looking for smaller patterns that can launch breakouts from larger patterns.

Companhia Siderurgica Nacional: 4-month descending flag

The last giant flag we'll look at is a set-up that I think Edwards & Magee would be interested in because it had a textbook classical pattern that formed after the breaking of the channel boundary. The next chart shows SID, a Brazilian steel maker, forming an intriguing double-pattern set-up:

FIGURE 57

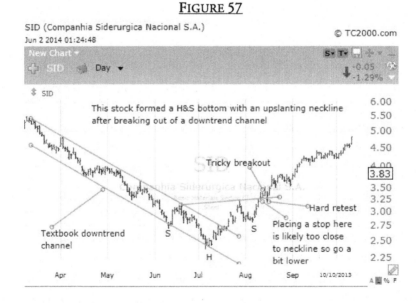

The eventual H&S bottom's left shoulder and half of the head formed inside the channel. The rest of the H&S bottom formed after prices broke above the upper boundary of the channel. Prices first closed above the neckline of the H&S bottom by the smallest of margins. After this hesitant breakout, prices seemed to gain momentum in the next two days to possibly start a strong run. Instead, three days after the indecisive breakout, prices plunged but did not close below the neckline in a difficult retest.

On the breakout day, there was very little trading below the neckline. Strictly applying the last day rule meant placing a stop just below the breakout day low, very close to the neckline and likely to be triggered by a hard retest or even normal volatility. In fact, the hard retest here triggered such a stop-loss order. So the specificities of this set-up and breakout called for modifying the last day rule to place our stop lower, say, somewhere below the closing price of the day before the breakout. Doing so still meant that we were risking only about 3% to 3.5% of our position to trade a very promising pattern. The next chart zooms in on the retest area:

FIGURE 57.1

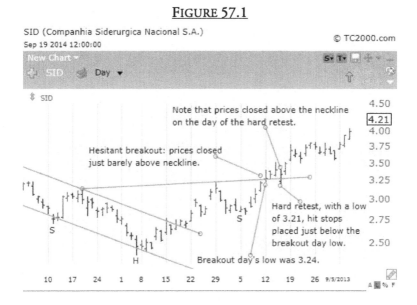

Let's say we were stopped out by the hard retest. Should we consider re-entering the trade? I think so. While prices plunged below the neckline at the beginning of the trading session, they decisively closed above the neckline at the end of the retest day. That prices closed above the neckline suggested the possibility that the pattern and breakout were still valid. It is important to understand that prices staying above the neckline did not guarantee anything as prices could plunge the next day. But the important thing was that this development provided a logical entry and exit set-up. We could buy shares around the closing price of the retest day and set our stop below the lowest reach of the hard retest. Again, there was no guarantee that another retest would not go farther below the first retest. But entering at this spot meant that our risk was defined and likely limited while the possible upside was greater. The stock made strong gains in the weeks and months following the hard retest.

CHAPTER 16
H&S Top Failure

As we started to discuss in Chapter 11, a H&S top failure pattern is when a stock forms a possible H&S top but rather than breaking down through the neckline it instead goes up and closes above the high of the right shoulder. A decisive close above the right shoulder can provide a buying opportunity.

<u>Avago Technologies: 3-month H&S top failure</u>

Let's first get a big-picture view of our next set-up. The next chart is a weekly chart that shows Avago Technologies doubling in price from the spring of 2010 to the spring of 2011 and then pausing and trading between the $30 and $40 range for the next two years:

FIGURE 58

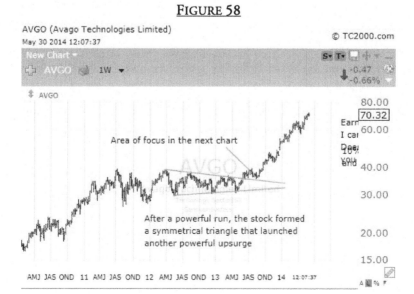

Avago Technologies formed a giant 14-month symmetrical triangle during the second half of this range-bound period. Let's now look at the daily chart that focuses on the breakout from the symmetrical triangle:

FIGURE 58.1

As we have learned, some breakouts are so powerful that they are untradeable, at least until another tradable pattern, such as a continuation pennant, forms. Here, the quarterly earnings report led to an unpredictable 10% jump and breakout from the giant symmetrical triangle. It was a decisive breakout, but it was not, in my opinion, a tradable breakout. I would not have bought shares even after the volatility surrounding the earnings release had passed because entering after the breakout meant risking close to 10% of my position. As of now, the set-up and breakout did not provide a favorable entry spot. And, as we know, we should not buy shares before the earnings release and hope that the market will react positively to the earnings news. This 10% increase could have been a 10%, 20%, or larger crash. Nobody knows how the market will react to earnings. We must wait and see how the chart plays out after the earnings report.

Two weeks after the breakout, a retest challenged but did not penetrate the upper boundary. Then stock traded between $35 and $40 for the next two months. There was no follow through after the explosive breakout. I have seen this scenario often and it is another reason why we must be very careful if we decide to chase a breakout. If we had bought a full-size position around the closing price of the breakout day, then we were likely to become very frustrated as prices stalled. We were susceptible to anxiously watching every price tick because we did not want to lose 10% of our position. As it is impossible to remain relaxed and detached while watching a stock's every move for days or weeks (let alone months), we get tired of waiting and sell, likely for a significant loss.

So if we are going to gamble and chase, we should use a significantly smaller position and place our stop-loss order at a reasonable distance away from upper boundary and then forget about the trade. No amount of wishing, hoping, and screen-gazing will make the trade work. Prices will take their time to do whatever they want to do.

Whether we decided to wait or buy a small position, we would have found three months after the breakout that not only had prices failed to break out of the congestion but also that a H&S top seemed to be forming. What was happening? How could a reversal pattern form so soon after what seemed like a decisive breakout from a giant 14-month symmetrical triangle? Of course patterns can fail anytime. And this once-promising set-up was now not only frustrating but also potentially very dangerous for those who were unwilling to accept the possibility that the pattern might fail.

Then we remember: every H&S top can become a H&S top failure. Every pattern can fail. A promising ascending triangle can fail and prices plunge down through the rising lower boundary instead of breaking through the horizontal upper boundary. An upside breakout from a rectangle can reverse and prices can shoot down through the upper boundary and then even the lower boundary. And so on. I have found H&S top and bottom failures to be particularly useful trading tools.

More trading opportunities result from knowing and being open to different possibilities. Charting is about possibilities. If the H&S top worked and prices broke down through the neckline and then the upper boundary of the giant symmetrical triangle, then we would conclude that the initial breakout was no longer valid and that the giant symmetrical triangle failed. If we had bought shares after the 10% jump, then we would be stopped out for a manageable loss. Whether we bought shares or not, we would move on.

Here, the H&S top failed and became a H&S top failure pattern when prices closed above the highest point of the right shoulder. An earnings reports led to the completion of the H&S top failure pattern just as it led to the breakout from the giant symmetrical triangle three months ago. If we had bought shares after the breakout from the symmetrical triangle, then we would have sold our shares before the latest earnings report to watch from the sidelines. Once the dust settled from the earnings release, we found that the H&S top failure pattern completed and created a good opportunity to re-enter the trade. And of course it was also a good opportunity to buy shares for the first time. We could buy shares around the closing price of the breakout and place a stop somewhere below the low and risk less than 1% of our position for a promising chart development. But, as always, patience was required. The stock traded in a very narrow range just above the right shoulder for two weeks before making a powerful run.

A clue that suggested that a H&S top failure pattern could develop was when the price decline in mid-August 2013 stayed above the support level established by the retest in mid-June. A H&S top pattern was still possible, but so was a H&S top failure pattern. Trading is all about being open to different possibilities and trading according to the actual price action rather than our wishes or biases. This chart was undeniably interesting: the 3-month congestion after the breakout from the symmetrical triangle took the form of a 3-month H&S top failure pattern, which finally launched the post-breakout follow through.

Whatever our initial approach to this set-up, patience was the vital ingredient for trading it well. We had to be patient while the giant symmetrical triangle developed and launched a breakout. We needed patience not to chase the initial breakout. If we chased the breakout with a small position, then we needed patience and discipline to get out before the next earnings report. And we needed to be patient after we entered the trade upon the H&S top failure. Be patient.

Crane Co.: 10-week H&S top failure

Let's again start with an overall view of the situation:

FIGURE 59

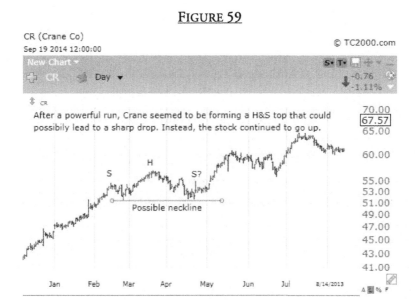

Crane Co. made a powerful run from 2012 into 2013 and then seemed to be possibly forming a significant H&S top pattern.

The next chart focuses on this possible H&S top pattern:

FIGURE 59.1

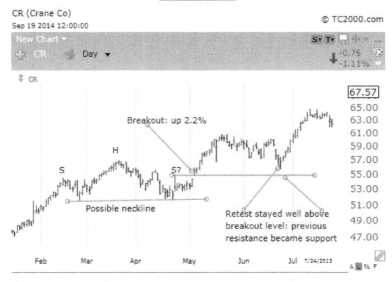

By the middle of April we saw a well-formed possible left shoulder and head as well as a horizontal neckline. By late April we also had a half-formed potential right shoulder. We were justified in suspecting a possible H&S top that might reverse the previous uptrend. But we also should have kept an open mind and remembered that every H&S top could become a H&S top failure. We had to stay mentally flexible and be willing to accept the actual price action. Such rules seem commonsensical but are often difficult to follow. Thus, we may have been jolted when prices closed above the possible right shoulder with a gap up in price. Not all price gaps are significant. For example, some thinly-traded stocks have price gaps almost daily. Here, however, the price gap seemed very significant because it occurred in a stock that had just a few price gaps in the last four months and it was the gap up that vaulted the stock above the right shoulder high. Thus, this gap up was very possibly a breakout gap that completed the H&S top failure pattern rather than simply a random price action.

This interpretation was supported by subsequent developments. First, prices made steady gains over the next three weeks. Second, prices stayed comfortably above the right-shoulder high when prices decline into late

June. It was now reasonable to conclude that the right-shoulder high had been a significant resistance level before the gap-up breakout and that now it had become a support level. **Previous resistance often becomes support, and prior support resistance**. We'll further discuss support and resistance in Chapter 21.

Facebook, Inc: 10-week H&S top failure

The next set-up combined a H&S top failure with an overlapping H&S pattern, another pattern that I learned from Peter L. Brandt:

FIGURE 60

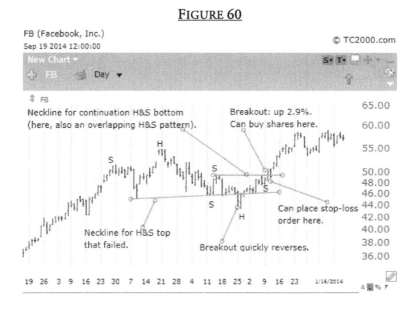

After making a strong run, Facebook formed a H&S top that seemed ready to push prices down. A decisive breakdown through the neckline seemed to complete the pattern and would have justified shorting shares. But the decline lasted only a day as prices reversed immediately and closed above the neckline within two days. Prices continued to go up, paused at the level of the right shoulder high, declined a bit, then burst through the right shoulder resistance level. The stock had completed a continuation

H&S bottom. Note how the right shoulder of the H&S top constituted the left shoulder and part of the head of the H&S bottom. Peter L. Brandt calls this an overlapping H&S pattern.

This price reversal need not alarm us. Yes, we would have lost money if we shorted Facebook shares upon the completion of the H&S top pattern. But our loss was nothing more than a minor one if we used prudent money management. We could have channeled our mild disappointment to finding other set-ups. And a good set-up could be found on the same chart less than two weeks later. In the process of forming a H&S top failure pattern, the chart also produced an overlapping H&S pattern, which was a small pattern that was easy to miss. We cannot and do not have to find every tradable pattern. Even if we could, we cannot and should not trade every one. Beginners, especially, should not worry about missing patterns. We will get better.

Kindred Healthcare: 6-month H&S top failure

The next set-up shows why it is so important yet sometimes so difficult to believe what we see rather than what we want to believe.

The following chart shows Kindred Healthcare doubling in price from summer 2012 to summer 2013 and then forming a possible H&S top from May to November 2013:

FIGURE 61

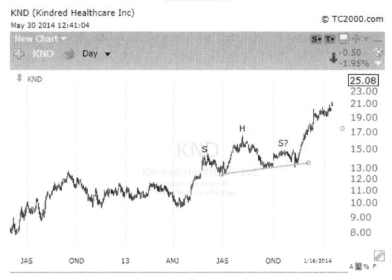

The next chart focuss on the possible H&S top that seemed poised to reverse the powerful uptrend:

FIGURE 61.1

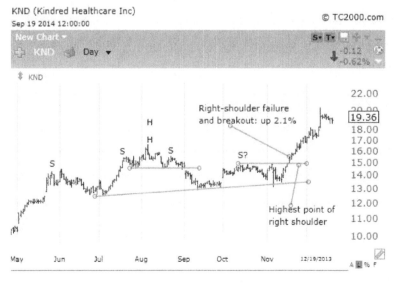

A well-defined H&S top was my first, second, and third impression. The symmetry of the left and right shoulders in duration, size, and shape was textbook. I also noticed that the head of this 5-month H&S top was itself a successful H&S top. I am always fascinated by such a pattern within a pattern. It was easy and comfortable to be committed to the H&S top interpretation. And it is fine to have an opinion. What is dangerous and costly is to be so attached to that opinion as to blind us from the actual price action. If we thought that a textbook H&S top was forming, then we had to re-evaluate the situation when prices decisively closed above the right shoulder high. This level was also the neckline of the small H&S top that formed the head of our beloved H&S top interpretation. It was also the high of the left shoulder. A decisive close above this significant level signaled the need to re-think our interpretation and trading strategy. If we had preemptively entered a short position, then we should have covered our position. If we were still waiting for the stock to break down through the neckline of the H&S top, then we should consider buying shares instead.

Experienced traders understand the importance of mental flexibility. It helps them overcome their biases and accept and trade the actual price action. Nimbleness allows them to recognize that the disappointing failure of a potentially textbook H&S top could mean a profitable trend in the other direction. Mental flexibility allows us to take advantage of a rapidly changing situation.

Extra Space Storage: 6-month H&S top failure

The next set-up also made it easy to believe that a trend reversal "had to happen." First the big-picture view of the situation:

FIGURE 62

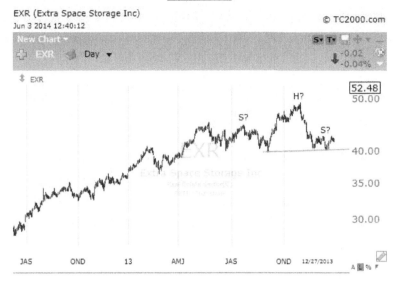

After doubling in price over 15 months, Extra Space Storage seemed to be forming a large H&S top that could reverse the uptrend.

The next chart focuses on the possible H&S top that was forming:

FIGURE 62.1

Prices did not break down through the neckline of the H&S top. Instead, the possible right shoulder of this seeming H&S top turned into a smaller continuation H&S bottom that launched another upswing. This set-up may also be called an overlapping H&S pattern.

CHAPTER 17
Double Bottom

Among the classical patterns, the double bottom (and double top) pattern is perhaps the most carelessly talked about price action. But Edwards & Magee laid out quite specific requirements for the double bottom and top, and true double bottoms and tops are rare.

One requirement is that the two bottoms be at least a month apart. Another is that the price increase between the first and second bottoms should be about 20%. Edwards & Magee said that the time requirement, that the bottoms be at least a month apart, is more important than the height of the rise and that most true double bottoms have bottoms that are two to three months apart. They also said that the greater the time between the two lows (or highs for a double top), the less important the requirement for a significant price increase (or decrease for a double top).

These requirements are not absolute and Edwards & Magee recognized that there are many examples that deviate from the textbook requirements. That said, we should try to adhere to the textbook requirements for double bottoms and tops as much as possible given that they are prone to much misuse and mislabel. My personal requirement for double bottoms and tops is that the two lows or peaks be at least two months apart.

NutriSystem: 7-month double bottom

Our only double bottom is one of my favoriate patterns from the last couple of years. It formed in NutriSystem from November 2012 to June 2013:

FIGURE 63

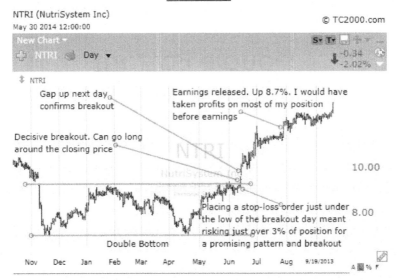

The two bottoms occurred five months apart, fulfilling the key requirement specified by Edwards & Magee. The price rise between the bottoms was almost 30%, meeting another requirement for a legitimate double bottom. The breakout was decisive and was followed the next day by a gap up.

There were two main challenges to trading this pattern well.

First, the wait: five months between the two bottoms and another two months until the breakout. A double bottom by definition does not form overnight. Some patterns, like flags, last only three or four days before starting a powerful run. In contrast, double bottoms reflect an extended process during which a stock's long-term downtrend reverses as buyers slowly accumulate shares from tired and sometimes demoralized sellers who have seen the stock lose a lot of its value over an extended period. Again, patience is the trader's best friend.

Second, diligence. We do not have to check every hour the progress of a potential double bottom. The skills required are long-term discipline and diligence: cycling through our stock list regularly over weeks and months as we look for good set-ups while keeping track of interesting developments such as a potential double bottom forming. We will talk more about our day-to-day routine in Chapter 28.

And if we missed the set-up and breakout? Let it go. There will always be other opportunities.

CHAPTER 18
Horn Bottom

A horn bottom is another interesting and useful though rare pattern. Edwards & Magee did not mention horns in their book but Richard Schabacker did in his. And Peter L. Brandt in his *Diary of a Professional Commodity Trader* specifies the requirements of a horn bottom: a major low followed by two higher lows intervened by two higher highs.

Sina Corp.: 7-month horn bottom

The following chart is a weekly chart that shows the overall set-up for our first horn bottom:

FIGURE 64

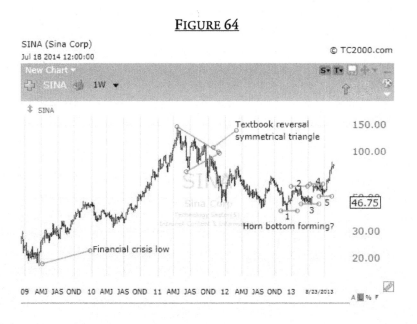

The stock went up more 7-fold from the financial crisis low in the spring 2009 to the spring of 2011, going from less than $20 a share to above $140 a share. Then it formed a 5-month reversal symmetrical triangle and lost more than 70% of its value over the next 20 months and was trading at about $40 a share in December 2012.

The next chart focuses on the horn bottom that formed after the December 2012 low:

FIGURE 64.1

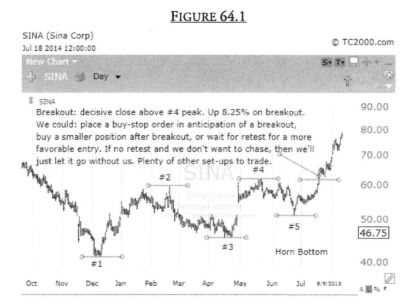

We have a major low (#1), followed by a peak (#2) and decline to a higher low (#3), and rally to a higher peak (#4) and another decline to a yet another higher low (#5). A key requirement is that there must be some overlap between the decline from #2 to #3 and the decline from #4 to #5. The pattern completed with a breakout above the second peak (#4).

I have found horn bottoms to be useful analytical and trading tools despite their relative rarity. When a stock is trading in a sort of range but its bottoms and peaks do not line up exactly as in a rectangle, I know that a horn pattern is an alternative and perhaps better interpretation. We must keep an open mind when analyzing the price action, and being aware of different possibilities helps us stay mentally flexible.

Gollinhas Aereas Inteligentes: 2-month horn bottom

Our next horn bottom was much smaller than our first but still produced a powerful trend. The next chart gives us the big-picture view:

FIGURE 65

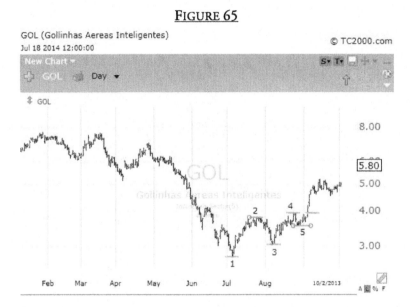

The stock was trading above $7.50 per share in the early months of 2013 before crashing to less than $2.75 per share by early July.

The next chart zooms in on the horn bottom pattern:

FIGURE 65.1

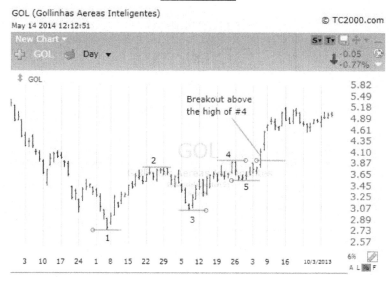

Note how this horn bottom fulfilled the pattern requirements. Just as important was the fact that this horn bottom formed where and when it was supposed to: after a long, disheartening price decline. A horn bottom is a reversal pattern. And reversal patterns need something to reverse, such as this long price decline.

CHAPTER 19
Diamond

The diamond is our next pattern. Diamonds can be continuation or reversal patterns. This versatility makes sense since the second half of a diamond pattern is a symmetrical triangle, and a symmetrical triangle can be either a continuation or reversal pattern.

Figure 66 provides the overall set-up surrounding a 6-month continuation diamond pattern in Susser Holdings:

FIGURE 66

Note the two-year reversal symmetrical triangle in the bottom left of Figure 66 that launched a big uptrend. After the stock gained more than 300% over the next two years, it paused and formed the following diamond pattern:

FIGURE 66.1

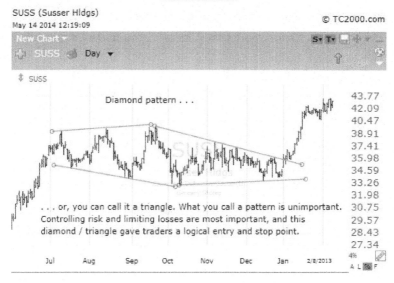

The next chart zooms in on the breakout area:

FIGURE 66.2

The upper boundary had five solid touches before prices finally closed above it. Buying shares around the closing price of the breakout day and placing a stop just below the low meant risking about 4% of our position. There was no immediate follow through as there was a hard retest the day after the breakout and prices traded near the boundary for a full week. Patience, as usual, was required.

Why not just call this set-up a symmetrical triangle? We can. After all, we would trade a breakout from a diamond in the same way as we would trade a breakout from a symmetrical triangle. I still think there is a good reason for charting this set-up as a 6-month diamond rather than a 3-month symmetrical triangle. The longer the consolidation or congestion period, the more likely it is that the breakout and ensuing trend will have staying power. A pattern's size is never a guarantee that a pattern will work well or work at all. But it is an important factor to consider when we are choosing among different set-ups. I'd rather tie up my money in a larger pattern with a larger measured price target than in a smaller pattern.

Diamond patterns are relatively rare. We will look at another textbook diamond pattern in Chapter 29.

CHAPTER 20
Second and Third Effort

Sometimes a stock breaks out only after several failed attempts. Let's take a look at the following ascending triangle that formed in United Community Banks:

FIGURE 67

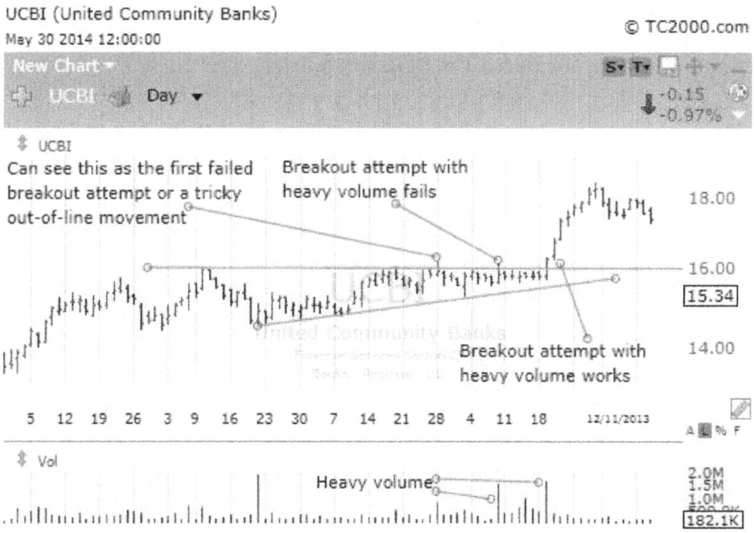

UCBI (United Community Banks)
May 30 2014 12:00:00
© TC2000.com

It is a small but relatively well-defined ascending triangle. I think the first "failed" breakout was just an out-of-line movement. So far we have seen so many textbook patterns with precise boundaries that it is easy to think that prices must stay within the lines we draw. But this example reminds us that patterns are not perfect. And they don't need to be to be useful trading tools. We must allow a certain amount of leeway as we draw patterns to make sense of the price action. Still, it is remarkable how often prices seem to respect our lines.

The stock tried to break out two weeks after the one-day out-of-line movement but was turned back. This failure could have been somewhat alarming to traders expecting an upside breakout given that the breakout failed on heavy volume. If a breakout could not be achieved on heavy volume, then perhaps the pattern was destined to not work. Such worrying is pointless as no one knows what prices will do. If the pattern fails, then so be it. The first failed breakout shows why it can be advantageous to wait before entering a trade. Most breakouts, even decisive ones, give traders time to enter at a favorable spot towards the end of the breakout day. The real breakout here, on the second attempt (or third attempt if we treat the out-of-line movement as a failed breakout), was decisive and buying shares around the closing price and placing a stop just below the low meant risking about 2.8% of our position.

Stay patient and wait for the pattern to prove itself.

CHAPTER 21
Support and Resistance

If I had describe the essence of good trading using the fewest words possible, then I would say "limit losses." If I were given up to five words, I would add "support and resistance."

The boundaries, horizontal or slanting, of all of the patterns we have analyzed are support and resistance levels. Breakouts go through support and resistance. Retests re-challenge support and resistance. Patterns fail when existing support and resistance levels fail. Charts evolve when new support and resistance levels form. And prior resistance often becomes support while prior support becomes resistance.

I find it amazing how well support and resistance levels perform their function. They don't work every time, but often enough to make classical charting possible and worthwhile. I also find it fascinating how support and resistance levels established years ago continue to work today.

The following examples show just how resilient support and resistance can be.

Chicago Bridge & Iron

The next chart is a weekly chart that shows the overall situation:

FIGURE 68

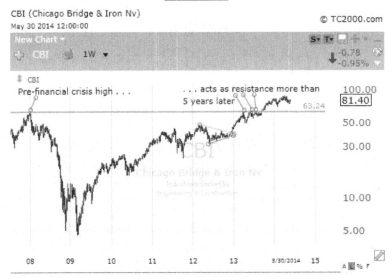

Note the pre-financial crisis high and how the stock lost more than 90% of its value over the next year. The stock recovered remarkably over the next four years and approached the pre-financial crisis high.

As we see in Figure 68.1, the stock tried to close above the old high reached more than five years ago. But heavy selling turned back the stock. Was the remarkable uptrend over or would the stock make another attempt to break above the old high?

FIGURE 68.1

CBI (Chicago Bridge & Iron Nv)
May 30 2014 12:00:00   © TC2000.com

New Chart

CBI   Day

CBI   81.40

Long-term resistance from
more than 5 years ago   Long-term resistance turns
                               back breakout attempts . . .   70.00

                                                                    63.24

                                                                             60.00

                    . . . while a symmetrical triangle forms that   50.00
                    leads to a breakout above resistance

        May   Jun   Jul   Aug   Sep   Oct   11/4/2013

The old-high-turned-resistance rejected another breakout try two months after the first attempt. And no tradable pattern seemed to be forming on the chart. But after another month, we saw that a possible symmetrical triangle was forming. Would the triangle reverse the 4-year uptrend or launch another uptrend?

Let's discuss how our emotions and prejudices, that is, being human, can affect our analysis and trading of this set-up. We now know that this symmetrical triangle launched another upleg to continue this incredible run. But let's try to get an honest sense of what our bias would have been if we were looking at this chart as it was developing. I'll tell you my bias. Very simply, I wanted the symmetrical triangle to reverse the 4-year uptrend and start a downtrend. I wanted a breakdown so much that I convinced myself that a trend reversal must happen because it was the right thing to happen. It was a case of believing what "had to happen" rather than the actual price action.

Why did I want the trend to reverse?

To be fair to myself, the stock did have an incredible run. Surely, I thought, the stock is too tired to start another uptrend. It failed twice, after all, to break above the all-time high establish five years ago. Going down would create a nice symmetry: two nice peaks 5 years apart that were both followed by momentous price declines. And, finally, haven't those lucky investors and traders in Chicago Bridge & Iron have had enough gains?

Let's examine this ridiculous yet, if you will allow, very human sentiment. **Money we did not make is not money we lost.** We will miss many set-ups that become big winners, but we don't lose money when we miss a trade. And nobody knew during unsettled days of the 2007-2009 financial crisis that Chicago Bridge & Iron would gain so much in the next 5 years. So why might we, and I'll shift to "we" from "I" because I don't want to be too harsh on myself, feel this way? Answer must be envy, no? We wanted that 14-fold gain. Never mind that almost everyone was too scared to go anywhere near the stock market during the financial crisis. Never mind that the company could have gone bankrupt and wiped out shareholders. Never mind that we might not have had the investing or trading skills then to take advantage of this "opportunity." Wishing we were part of this huge gain is like wishing we bought Microsoft shares in 1986 when the company went public. In short, it is a silly and juvenile wallowing in fantasy.

We must always try to prevent our emotions from blinding us from the actual price action. But we are human, and thus we have a remarkable ability to ignore reality. I did not believe my eyes when the textbook symmetrical triangle produced a decisive breakout to the upside with immediate follow through. So I did not buy the breakout. I watched the stock go up and up and waited for the stock to crash because it "had to" go down. My hope is that this example of my strenuous ignorance will motivate others to always be on guard against their emotions. Believe what you see, not what you want to believe.

Another lesson is that sometimes a stock will break out of a classical pattern before breaking through a long-term resistance or support level. I compare it to an airplane slowly building up speed to gather the energy and momentum to get airborne. We saw such a build-up in the flag pattern formed by Clearwater Paper Corp., discussed in Chapter 15, that launched a breakout through multi-month resistance.

Johnson & Johnson

Here's another example of stock gathering momentum for a breakout. First, let's look at the weekly chart to get an overall sense of the situation:

FIGURE 69

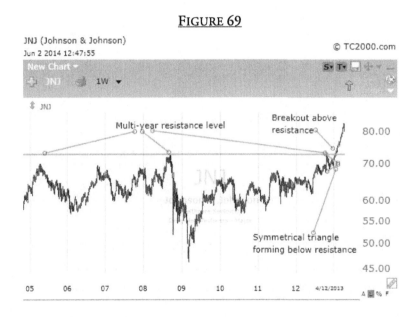

The next chart focuses on the 2-month symmetrical triangle that formed just under the resistance level on the right side of Figure 69:

FIGURE 69.1

JNJ (Johnson & Johnson)
Jun 2 2014 01:11:33

© TC2000.com

Note the textbook symmetrical triangle and breakout. But how to deal with the looming earnings release? If we had bought shares around the closing price of the breakout day, then we were sitting on about a 3% profit the day before the earnings report. We should exit our position for a modest profit and move on. Because Johnson & Johnson is a relatively stable stock with a strong financial position based on a rock-solid business, we could argue that there is a stronger case for holding a small position through earnings. Even a negative market reaction to earnings probably won't crash the stock by much. However, while Johnson & Johnson is a solid company, we must still be prudent and not gamble on earnings.

In any event, the lesson here is not how to trade through earnings. Our policy towards earnings remains the same: do not trade through earnings, and, if we do, we do so with a drastically scaled-down position that will not hurt us much if the stock crashes on earnings. The real takeaway is to look for patterns that may form near powerful resistance and support levels.

Seagate Technology

Our final chart of this chapter shows again the importance and ubiquitousness of support and resistance, and how previous support can become resistance and vice versa:

FIGURE 70

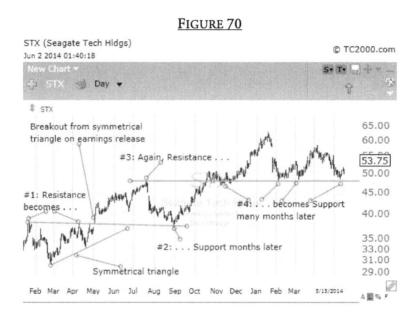

Support and resistance levels don't always work, but they work well enough to be more than mere coincidence and to serve as a foundation of classical charting and prudent trading. And when they don't work, our stop-loss orders will exit us from the trade for a minor loss.

Trying to find the perfect trading system, one that guarantees that most trades will make money, can be irresistible, especially when we are on a losing streak. That is the wrong approach and almost certainly will lead to bigger losses. Returning to the basics, such as never chasing a breakout and focusing on support and resistance, is the most fruitful thing to do when we are suffering through a losing streak. We have to remember and accept the fact that losing streaks are part of trading. All traders experience them. But the best traders trade in a way that even 20, 30, or more losses in a row will not drain their trading account by much.

CHAPTER 22
Pattern within a Pattern

We have already looked at many pattern-within-pattern set-ups. I think they are so interesting and useful that we should devote a separate chapter to them.

Boeing

The next chart is a weekly chart that shows a 15-month continuation H&S bottom in Boeing:

FIGURE 71

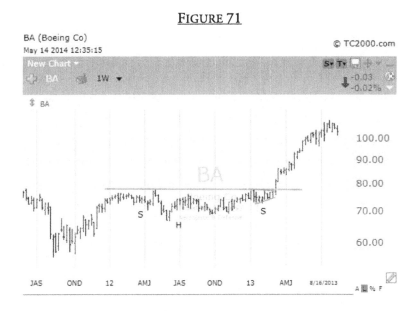

FIGURE 71

Boeing made strong gains from the second half of 2011 to early 2012. Then it stalled for 14 months as it could not break above the $78 level. By early 2013, it seemed Boeing had been forming an intriguing continuation H&S bottom with an abbreviated right shoulder.

The next chart is a daily chart that focuses on right portion of this possible continuation H&S bottom:

FIGURE 71.1

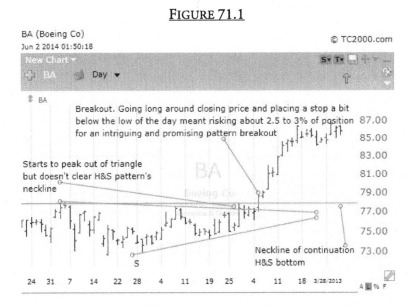

The right shoulder of this continuation H&S bottom developed in the form a 2-month symmetrical triangle. We had several opportunities to enter this trade. We could buy shares as soon as the stock closed above the upper boundary of the symmetrical triangle. Or, we could have waited until the stock decisively broke above the horizontal neckline of the continuation H&S bottom. We could have entered even a day after the breakout through the neckline.

We should always look for smaller patterns that can start the breakout from a larger pattern. Patterns like this symmetrical-triangle right shoulder can help us understand the overall price action and even provide an earlier opportunity to enter the trade. We have to keep our minds open with a creative mindset to take advantage of these additional clues.

One of the best ways to stay mentally flexible is to be always drawing different trendlines and boundaries to see the various ways to make sense of the price action. Just as it is crucial to write down our ideas or risk forgetting them and lose the chance to develop them later, drawing pattern boundaries using our charting program helps us understand the price action and also helps us spot and keep track of emerging patterns. This monitoring-function is very important. While the initial boundaries we draw will often need to be redrawn as patterns evolve, they can also work from the beginning. We are less likely to miss breakouts from the more modest-sized patterns, like this two-month symmetrical triangle, if we have already framed the price action with our drawings.

Sabra Healthcare

Here's our next pattern within a pattern. First, let's get a big-picture view:

FIGURE 72

After making strong gains throughout 2012, Sabra Healthcare took a break from its strong uptrend and traded in a relatively tight range from

November to December 2012. This range-bound price action produced an ascending triangle and a smaller symmetrical triangle within it.

The next chart zooms in on the patterns:

FIGURE 72.1

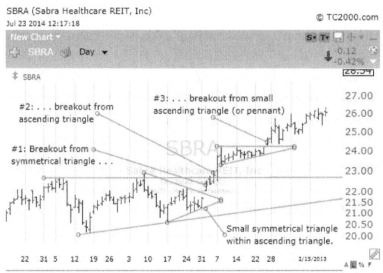

The breakout from the small symmetrical triangle led to the breakout from the larger ascending triangle. The first breakout did not guarantee that the ascending triangle would work. The breakout could have reversed and the chart could have continued to evolve into something else entirely. The breakout from the small symmetrical triangle had no inherent meaning, did not represent some universal truth, and did not guarantee anything. It is merely one possible interpretation of the price action to help us find advantageous entry and exit points. We could have bought shares on the day of the breakout from the symmetrical triangle on the expectation that a breakout from the larger ascending triangle would follow. In this case, that possibility came true and we were rewarded for our interpretation of the price action. If the first breakout turned out to be a meaningless price gap and the pattern failed, then we were out with a small loss. But we should not be too disappointed because we had made a worthwhile bet. We move on.

Note that we had another chance to buy shares even if we missed both breakouts. If we patiently refused to chase the missed breakouts and monitored the chart over the next couple of works, we saw a 2-week ascending triangle develop. The breakout from this small continuation pattern provided another favorable entry spot. The lesson: there will always be more opportunities.

Goodyear Tire & Rubber

Our next example was not the prettiest pattern but it can still teach us important lessons. Figure 73 is a weekly chart showing the overall set-up:

FIGURE 73

The next chart is a daily chart that focuses on the last five months of this 16-month symmetrical triangle:

FIGURE 73.1

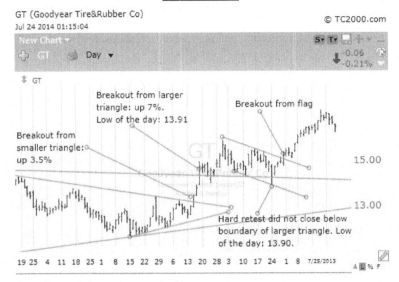

A 5-week symmetrical triangle formed inside the 16-month symmetrical triangle. A decisive breakout from this small triangle led to a breakout from the larger triangle.

Note the big advantage given to traders who bought shares upon the breakout from the small triangle. They risked around 3.5% of their position and would enjoy larger profits given their earlier entry. In contrast, we had to risk about 7% of our position when buying shares after the breakout from the larger triangle. Quite simply, in this set-up, if we missed the breakout from the small triangle, then we had to risk more, work harder, and be more patient to trade the pattern well. Some of us may hesitate risking 7% of our position. Thus, we may decide to not trade this set-up. Of course we can use a smaller position, and that's what I would have done had I missed the first breakout.

Once we decided on the size of our position, then our work was just beginning.

Let's say we bought shares upon the breakout from the larger triangle and set our stop just below the breakout day's low. A hard retest occurred four days later when the stock penetrated deep below the upper boundary but did not close below it. Another retest occurred two week later but this retest did not penetrate the upper boundary. The most challenging retest occurred another two weeks later when the stock again traded deep into the pattern. The lowest reach of this hard retest was 13.89. The low of the breakout from the symmetrical triangle was 13.91. If we had set our stop-loss order at 13.90, a penny below the breakout day's low, then we got stopped out. I usually give a bit more leeway to my stop-loss order, say, in the range of two to five cents. But it's possible that I could have used just a penny-buffer given that I was already risking 7% or more of my position.

Let's say that this third retest stopped us out. We notice that the stock seemed to just barely close above the upper boundary at day's end. What to do now?

Here are some of our choices:

First, we can move on. We bet on a good set-up and breakout and we got stopped out by a deep retest. We move on because we know there are many more promising set-ups. Those of us who like to keep trades on a short leash will like this option. We simply move on if we get stopped out and almost never re-enter a trade after getting stopped out.

Second, we can buy shares around the closing price of the third retest and set our stop just below that day's low. We are giving this trade another shot on the rationale that this third retest could be the low point of this post-breakout congestion because the stock closed above, albeit only slightly, the upper boundary of the symmetrical triangle. Another attempt meant risking 2.4% of our position, a very manageable loss, especially if we were stopped out on a smaller-than-usual position.

Another option is to wait and look for another tradable classical pattern to develop.

Within a few days of the third retest we saw that it was possible to interpret this entire post-breakout congestion as a descending flag. We can buy shares upon breakout from this descending flag.

Like all charts, there is no single correct way to trade this set-up. Besides the fact that buying the breakout from the smaller triangle worked best and imposed the least stress on us, our personalities and trading styles will determine how, or, even whether, to trade this set-up. Managing risk is our top duty. **We shouldn't be afraid to pass on a chart just because the set-up is intriguing.** There will always be other promising trades. If we decided to trade this set-up, then several significant technical developments (a pattern within a pattern, decisive breakouts, and prices that did not close below the upper boundary despite hard retests) suggested that it could be worthwhile to devote extra attention to this set-up.

Cheniere Energy

Our next example features a continuation H&S bottom within a larger symmetrical triangle:

FIGURE 74

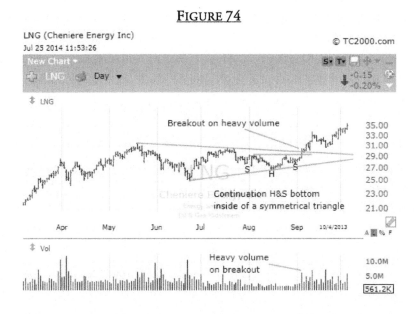

The symmetrical triangle had textbook form, and the smaller continuation H&S bottom also had good structure. The breakout from the H&S bottom coincided with the breakout from the symmetrical triangle. Buying shares around the closing price of the breakout day and placing a stop-loss order just below the low meant risking just above 4% for a promising double breakout. The volume spike on breakout increased the likelihood that the breakout would work. In this case, the smaller pattern did not provide an early entry opportunity.

Tesla Motors

Our next example reminds us of the thornier aspects of trading. We must remember that a decisive breakout from a promising pattern does not necessarily provide an advantageous trade opportunity. Let's again see why.

The next chart is a weekly chart that shows Tesla breaking out of a massive 2-year ascending triangle:

FIGURE 75

The next chart is a daily chart focusing on the last part of this ascending triangle:

FIGURE 75.1

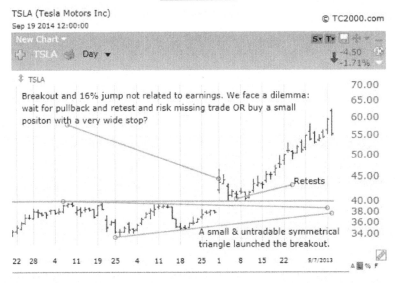

A 7-week symmetrical triangle formed at the very end of the ascending triangle. We saw in Chapter 21 how a stock can form a classical pattern just below a powerful resistance level in preparation for a possible breakout. The horizontal upper boundary of this giant ascending triangle was also a multi-year resistance level that, unsurprisingly, was not easily overcome. Traders were understandably excited when they spotted this symmetrical triangle developing just under resistance. An upside breakout from this small symmetrical triangle could launch a breakout from the larger ascending triangle and perhaps even provide an early opportunity to buy shares.

The breakout was decisive. So decisive, jumping 16%, that buying shares after the breakout was problematic. What should we do? Here are some of our options:

First, we could decide not to buy shares unless prices came back down. We wait for a retest that will provide an entry that will allow us to risk less of our position. No matter how promising the set-up and how potentially explosive the uptrend, we don't have to trade if we decide that the nature of the breakout makes the trade too risky. Here, the retest brought down prices exactly to the upper boundary. Previous resistance was now support.

We were given a chance to buy shares at a spot with a much more favorable reward-to-risk ratio. Of course waiting for a retest that might not have happened meant risk missing the trade entirely. **But it is perfectly okay to miss a trade. What is bad is being obsessed about not missing a trade.** So if there had been no retest, then we move on. Never hastily and recklessly chasing a breakout, and thus sometimes "missing" a breakout, is the price we must happily pay to not squander our capital on suboptimal set-ups.

Second, we could buy a small position that keeps our potential loss within our normal risk parameters. If there is no retest and the stock surges higher, then we make money. If there is a retest, then we might consider adding to our small position, still making sure to stay under our maximum risk.

We always have a choice. We never have to chase breakouts. And sometimes waiting means we get a better deal.

CHAPTER 23
Pattern Failures and Mutations

When we look back at the charts we have analyzed, we may justifiably be impressed with classical charting's usefulness as a trading tool. So useful and intriguing that we may also be tempted to think of classical charting as a mathematical certainty or science. We must avoid this mistake. Classical charting is not an exact science. It does not and cannot predict or guarantee anything. Nothing related to investing or trading is certain, except risk. The more fervent the claim of certainty, the more skeptical we must be. We must also have a healthy dose of skepticism with experts' opinions, claims, and predictions. Always remember that we don't have to do anything with our money just because somebody says we should. Nobody, including the experts, knows much about future economic and stock market performance. Consider the following instance.

The global financial crisis starting in 2007 was the most serious economic challenge since the Great Depression of the 1930s. Yet financial writer Tim Harford points out that economists as a group failed to forecast this economic disaster. In fact, as late as September 2008, the expert consensus was that not a single country among the 77 being examined would be in recession in 2009. Forty-nine countries were in a recession in 2009. America suffered its deepest economic downturn since the Great Depression and many argue that we are still far from full recovery.

The lesson is that we must not blindly follow others, even our mentors. **Trading offers great freedom but also demands much responsibility**. We must do our own thinking. In addition to treating expert pronouncements with due caution, we must apply the same care and prudent skepticism to our trading. There are no guarantees in trading. Patterns fail often.

To emphasize the fact that patterns are prone to change and failure and **we should never rely on classical charting as a precise forecasting tool**, this chapter will focus on set-ups that did not work. Looking at the following failed patterns will remind us why we must always use stop-loss orders and diversify our trades. Indeed, a trader's assumption on every trade should be that it will fail. No amount of wishing and fantasizing will make a trade profitable. We can only control where we enter and how much we risk. And by risking only a small fraction of our capital on each trade, we can trade for the long run.

Texas Industries

Figure 76 shows a H&S top with a slightly up-sloping neckline:

FIGURE 76

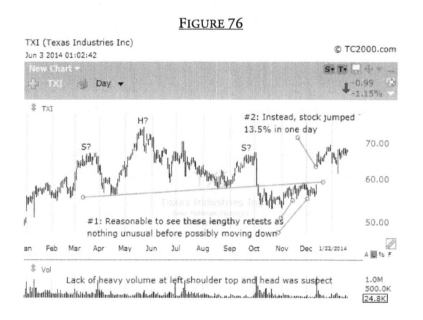

We also have a decisive breakdown through the neckline. The stock traded in a narrow range for two months and then gapped up 13.5% in early December. If we shorted this stock after the breakdown through the neckline, we lost 15% or more of our position when price surged up and we were stopped out.

Several takeaways here.

First, we must always diversify our trades. A stock can crash or jump for any or no reason. Price gaps happen. The 13.5% spike here was unrelated to an earnings report. Prices just jumped. Thus, we must never bet our entire stake on one trade or even several trades.

Second, we can lose more than we had planned. If we shorted this stock after the breakdown through the neckline and placed a buy-to-cover stop-loss order just above the high of the breakout day, we meant to risk about 5% of our position. But reality can have other plans, and our loss was three times greater than what we were willing to risk.

Third, it is okay to occasionally lose more than we had allowed for due to price gaps and unexpected news. No amount of careful risk management can account for unpredictable price gaps. But we can and must always diversify our trades so that a huge unfavorable price move remains a very manageable loss.

Fourth, one could argue that volume did not support a H&S top interpretation. The textbook specifies very heavy volume at the left shoulder peak and head. This possible H&S top did not have such climatic volume at the peaks. That said, volume is only one factor in my analysis, and I would have shorted the breakdown through the neckline given the pattern's good form and meaningful decline through a significant support level.

Fifth, after breaking down through the neckline, the stock traded in a narrow range for 10 weeks. Is that too long to wait for a follow through after the initial breakout? Hard to say. Patience is a vital trading skill. And some set-ups need time to work. Some traders use a time-stop along with a price stop. They exit the trade even if their stop-loss order has not been triggered if the stock does not start working in their favor within a certain period.

Lastly, we should stay nimble and be open to trading in the opposite direction from the anticipated breakout. After the H&S top failed in Texas

Industries, the chart could evolve and produce another tradable pattern, such as a H&S top failure pattern. But we will miss such an opportunity if we are preoccupied with being disappointed with the failure of the H&S top. Powerful trends in the other direction often come from failed breakouts. That said, it is understandable if traders who suffered a 15% loss on their short position simply want to move on to other opportunities. Mental flexibility is important, but more important is clearing our minds and moving on from a loss. If we dwell on the "unfairness" of the price jump in Texas Industries that resulted in our losing much more than we had carefully allotted for, then we will dwell on making our money back from this chart. The stock, after all, "owes" us. So we start trading even if there is no compelling set-up and we lose more money. The stock now owes us more money so we keep trading and lose more money. The destructive cycle continues and we suffer more financial and psychological pain. **As we know, many life lessons apply to trading. Moving on after a setback is one of them.**

Basic Energy Services

Our next example combines a pattern failure and a pattern evolution. Figure 77 shows a failed breakout from a symmetrical triangle:

FIGURE 77

BAS (Basic Energy Services Inc)
May 16 2014 12:00:00

© TC2000.com

Textbook pennant inside larger triangle. Looks very promising . . .

But breakout fails and stock drops 11% on earnings release

In addition to its good shape, this symmetrical triangle in Basic Energy also had a small pennant that formed just below the upper boundary that might launch a powerful breakout from the larger triangle – the always interesting pattern within a pattern. The breakout from the pennant was initially powerful. But the upward momentum died quickly and the stock decisively closed below the upper boundary of the triangle three days later, which was one day before the earnings release. The stock dropped 11% on earnings news. The bullish breakout from the symmetrical triangle failed completely.

So was that it? Should we move on? Yes, for now. But we would also periodically check in on Basic Energy as part of our regular cycling through of our charts.

Before examining how the chart evolved in the following months, let's discuss one more thing about this symmetrical triangle interpretation. Was there a meaningful breakout from the symmetrical triangle? We have discussed how some traders do not consider a breakout from a symmetrical triangle or any pattern with a slanting boundary to be an entry signal unless the breakout decisively closes above a significant high within the pattern (for a long trade such as here) or closes below a significant low (for a short trade).

The following chart illustrates this point:

FIGURE 78

As we discussed, I don't think there is a single best way to trade breakouts from patterns with slanting boundaries. Determining what constitutes an entry signal will depend on our risk tolerance, personality, and trading style. I would have bought shares upon the breakout from the symmetrical triangle but exited my position when the breakout could not quickly close above the horizontal resistance level. The next quarterly earnings report was to be released in three days and it was better to exit with little or no loss or even a small profit rather than hope that the stock quickly overcome a strong resistance level and make a meaningful run in a mere three days.

Now, let's discuss the chart's evolution after the failure of the symmetrical triangle. Two months later, we saw that the chart was forming a possible descending wedge:

FIGURE 78.1

BAS (Basic Energy Services Inc)
Jul 25 2014 12:00:00
© TC2000.com

New Chart ▾

BAS   Day ▾   -2.49   -8.96%

BAS

Breakout from flag but I wouldn't enter here because earnings release is 4 days later.

Breakout from descending wedge 2 days after earnings released.

Continuation symmetrical triangle

20.00

15.00

Flag within descending wedge

Symmetrical triangle failed, then became a descending wedge that worked.

eb Mar Apr May Jun Jul Aug Sep Oct Nov Dec   2/18/2014   A ▯ % F

In addition to the wedge, a possible descending flag was forming inside the descending wedge. As we know that a small pattern can launch a breakout from the larger pattern, we would carefully watch this chart.

The flag produced a decisive breakout. I still would not have bought shares because the next earnings report was due four days later. I would buy shares after the earnings release and after a decisive breakout from the descending wedge, which occurred on October 29. If we had bought shares on October 29, we were up by almost 34% by November 8. A great gain even if we bought only a small position. And the size of the descending wedge indicated that even larger gains were possible.

Very few breakouts go straight up or down. And every set-up presents unique challenges. Here, sitting on a 34% profit, should we continue to hold? I wouldn't blame anyone for taking at least partial profits at this point.

Let's say that we decide to take profits on one-third of our position and hold the rest. Over the next month we watched the profits in our remaining position evaporate as the stock declined and tried to retest the upper boundary of the descending wedge.

This retest shows perfectly why trading challenges so much our mental and physical strength. We know that retests are normal and that all breakouts are subject to pauses and even outright failure. We also know that all we can do is to enter at a favorable spot, set our stop, and move aside. But knowing our limitations is one thing. Accepting them to achieve calm and mental clarity is much more difficult. We could suspect that this price decline indicated that the pattern and breakout were about to fail. Many of us are likely to sell our remaining shares in frustration at the early December lows, after all of our profits have disappeared, as we don't want to lose any more money. So we sell and stop paying attention to this chart. We hate the chart because it didn't go straight up. We don't care whether the retest is over or how the chart may evolve in the coming weeks.

But consider the attitude of experienced traders who bought the breakout on October 29 and used the last day rule to set their stop-loss order just below the low of the breakout day. The price decline into early December did not come close to triggering their stops. The decline turned out to be a relatively weak retest that did not even threaten touching the upper boundary of the descending wedge. Of course no one could know how sharp the retest would be. All anyone could do is enter, set their stop, and move on to other charts and projects. They could have been stopped out and lose all the profits they were sitting on in early November plus some more. There is no way to preclude this possibility. Patterns can fail no matter how decisive the breakout or beautiful the set-up. Our profits can evaporate in days or even seconds. The sooner we accept this reality of trading, the quicker we can start to trade in a calm and detached manner focusing on doing the right things rather than making money. Here, the early-December lows turned out to be the lowest point of the retest. The stock went on to form and break out of a 2-month continuation symmetrical triangle.

The formation of this textbook symmetrical triangle shows again why we must regularly review our charts. A quick and focused view couple of times a week would have alerted us to the forming of a possible symmetrical triangle. This triangle gave another chance to buy shares if we had missed the breakout from the descending flag or descending wedge or if we sold our position in early November. Also, those patiently holding since the flag breakout could add to their position and move up their stops to the breakout from the symmetrical triangle. We still had to be patient even after the decisive breakout from the textbook continuation symmetrical triangle. The stock traded in a narrow range for 3 weeks before surging higher.

We should not worry if we feel a bit overwhelmed by the many evolutions that the Basic Energy chart went through. We do not have to catch every or even most intriguing charts. We just need to trade well a couple of set-ups. And if we lose on the few set-ups that we catch, then we know that there will always be more set-ups to come.

Altria Group

Our next example is a 3-month H&S top that formed inside an 18-month ascending wedge:

FIGURE 79

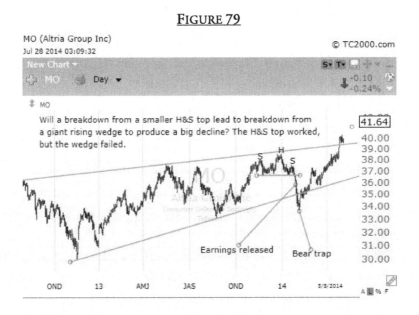

Both patterns had good structure. Especially interesting was how the head of the H&S top stayed just below the upper boundary of the rising wedge. The stock broke down decisively through the H&S top's neckline. The next day the stock plunged as the market reacted negatively to the quarterly earnings report. In two more days, the stock decisively closed below the lower boundary of the ascending wedge. Traders had good reason to consider shorting shares at this point.

The stock declined a bit more before pausing and surging higher to do a hard retest of the lower boundary. The stock traded around the lower boundary of the wedge for several weeks before surging higher. It closed above the neckline of the H&S top and eventually broke above the upper boundary of the ascending wedge.

A promising set-up that failed decisively. Why study failed set-ups? To remind ourselves that many, if not most, patterns will fail. We have looked at many ideal set-ups with clean breakouts. And many of our trades will be like these set-ups and work well. But many will not. Many will test us before working or failing. We must try our best to remain above the volatility and focus on trading well rather than trying to make money. The best way to focus on doing what's right is to enter at a favorable spot, set our stop, and move on. We have no control over whether a trade works. We can only manage our risk. **These are blindingly obvious statements but we tend to forget these truths when we bet real money**. Experienced traders have learned to maintain a calm state of mind no matter what happens in the markets. The best way to try to stay detached from the gyrations of the markets is to risk only a small portion of our account on any individual trade. If we do this, even our worst case scenario will be manageable.

I think this failed ascending wedge asks an important question: should we have traded it at all? Was the set-up promising to begin with? This question makes clear that **knowing when not to trade is just as important as how we trade.**

Let's examine the set-up again. The H&S top had good shape and the breakdown through the neckline was decisive. But how tradable was this breakdown? We would have been prudent to not trade it given that the quarterly earnings report was released the day after the stock closed below the neckline. And as the stock continued to decline in the days following the earnings report, it did not offer a favorable spot to short shares. We essentially "missed" the breakout, by choice, because of the pending earnings news. Entering now, so far below the neckline, meant risking too much.

Did we have a better spot to short shares after the stock closed below the lower boundary of the ascending wedge? Perhaps, but we had to remember the additional difficulty trading patterns with slanting boundaries. Due to the rising lower boundary, a retest here meant that the stock could stay under the lower boundary of the ascending wedge and still trigger our stop order. A hard retest did happen and would have stopped out our short position.

Shorting shares upon the breakdown through the lower boundary of the ascending wedge would not have been a bad trade. My point is that this set-up was not so ideal after all, especially since we did not have a good opportunity to enter earlier via the breakdown from the H&S top. And because of the drawbacks of this set-up, it would have been more than reasonable to simply pass on this trade no matter how interesting the pattern-within-a-pattern set-up. Remember, not all breakouts are tradable. We should trade only the most desirable among the tradable breakouts. The more experience I gain in the markets, the more I find myself passing on patterns that I would have traded in the past. I have learned to be more patient (don't get me wrong – it is a constant struggle) because experience has taught me that there always be more and better set-ups. Such knowledge helps me remain calm and patient more often than not.

CHAPTER 24
Do Not Gamble on Earnings Reports

As we have discussed many times so far, we should avoid trading through earnings reports. I almost always exit my entire position in a stock that is about to release its quarterly earnings report. Only rarely, and only if I'm sitting on a profit, will I keep a small position through an earnings release.

I avoid trading earnings reports even though I know that exiting my position can mean "missing" huge gains if the market reacts positively to the earnings news. The following example shows the kinds of gains we might "miss" if we always exit our position before earnings announcements:

FIGURE 80

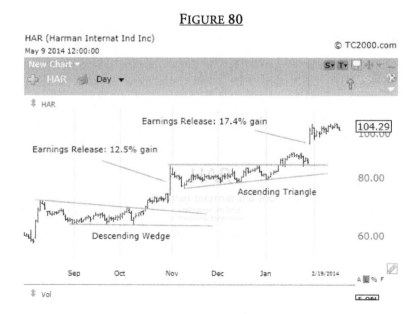

So then why should we not hold positions through earnings reports? We know the answer. Because stocks can crash on earnings news as well:

FIGURE 81

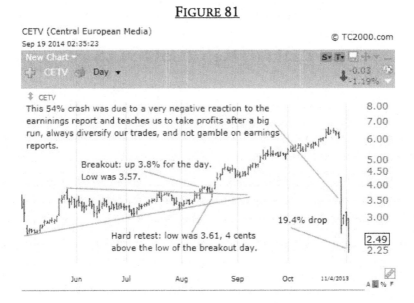

CETV (Central European Media)
Sep 19 2014 02:35:23   © TC2000.com

New Chart ▾   S▾ T▾
CETV Day ▾   -0.03
                                                     -1.19%

↕ CETV
This 54% crash was due to a very negative reaction to the   8.00
earninings report and teaches us to take profits after a big   7.00
run, always diversify our trades, and not gamble on earnings   6.00
reports.
                                                                   5.00
    Breakout: up 3.8% for the day.   4.50
    Low was 3.57.   4.00
                                                                   3.50
                                                    19.4% drop   3.00

    Hard retest: low was 3.61, 4 cents   2.49
    above the low of the breakout day.   2.25

    Jun   Jul   Aug   Sep   Oct   11/4/2013
                                                                  A ▦ % F

We analyzed this CETV chart in Chapter 11. It is foolish to risk a significant portion of our capital on a blind luck of the draw. Such outright gambling is simply unnecessary. We study classical charting because it allows us to take calculated risks at only advantageous spots. And we saw entry points with highly favorable reward-to-risk possibilities where we must risk only about 2-3% of our position. Steadily building our capital is the goal. Overnight successes are based on extremely rare luck, and such luck is often based on reckless gambles that wiped out all except the few that we hear about as overnight successes.

We are human, and therefore we are impatient and greedy. We want money, preferably a lot of it, today or at the latest tomorrow. We are not going to get it. We know that there is no easy road to success anywhere; we just don't want to believe it. We should play the long game while steadily gaining experience and capital. I strongly believe that trading is all about longevity. By protecting our capital against large losses, we can trade for the long run. And long-term survival greatly increases the chance that we will make it simply by virtue of the almost inevitable coming together of acquired wisdom and favorable market conditions.

Sometimes the market will have very few charts that look promising. But there will always be periods when the market throws us many fat pitches to choose from. These ideal pitches and the large potential profits are the result of impatient traders who spent their capital chasing poor set-ups and treacherous curveballs. Now they are too spent, financially and mentally, to take measured swings at the fat pitches. But we can take advantage if we have carefully preserved our financial and mental capital through patience and discipline.

CHAPTER 25

Being Out of Position: Not Trading No Matter How Promising the Set-Up and Breakout

We know that not all breakouts are tradable. We saw some breakouts that are so powerful that it was too risky to enter after the breakout. I call this situation being **out of position**. When we are out of position, we should not chase, no matter how tempting and promising the pattern. If we recklessly chase, then we must mitigate the potential damage by using a much smaller position to avoid getting caught in a negative feedback loop of chasing, losing money, chasing, and losing more money.

Flir Systems

The next chart shows Flir Systems breaking out of a well-defined symmetrical triangle:

FIGURE 82

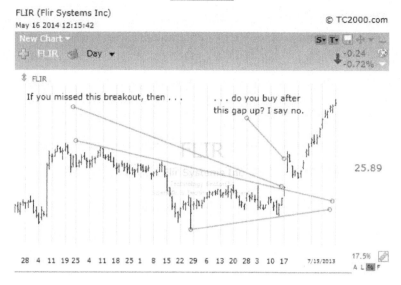

Note the first time prices closed above the upper boundary. While the stock did not close above the upper boundary of the symmetrical triangle by a large margin, it did so clearly, at least to my eyes. I would have bought shares at this point. The fact that this breakout was through a boundary with three good touches would be a factor in my buying. Perhaps the most important factor was that I would be risking only about 2% of my position to buy shares at this point. The potential upside was great while the downside was very manageable.

Others will disagree with my analysis. Some of us will prefer a more decisive breakout that closed above the prior significant high. Because there was no such breakthrough here, we may have decided to wait for a stronger breakout confirmation. That decision is a very reasonable one regardless of what happened next.

The next day the stock jumped more than 6%. If we didn't enter the day before, should we buy shares now?

My opinion is that if we did not buy shares at the initial breakout, then we should not chase this jump unless prices came back down and retested the upper boundary of the triangle to provide us a much more favorable entry spot. Entering after the 6% jump meant having to risk up to 8-9% of our position and I think that is too much.

Prices did come back down but not enough for me to enter this trade. Entering now meant buying shares when I was clearly out of position. I still could chase with a much smaller position but I prefer not to. And I try to never chase a breakout using a full position because the consequence is almost always emotional and financial pain.

But let's say that we chased using our regular-size position after the 6% jump. If the stock continued to surge higher, then we got lucky and made a large profit. But remember that making money is very different from trading well and doing the right thing. Anybody can get lucky occasionally. More often we are not so lucky. The stock could have reversed just after we bought shares and decline all the way down to the pattern boundary in a perfectly normal retest. Here, there was a retest that declined halfway to the boundary. If we did not set our stop low enough after chasing the 6% jump, then we would have been stopped out and would watch as prices surged higher without us. We would be frustrated and angry, and we may chase again. When we again buy shares, the stock may pause and reverse yet again to stop us out. It is a painful cycle of financial loss and mental pain. It gets increasingly difficult to move on from the crushing combination of damaged pride (why couldn't I make money on this trade?), greed (I thought I was going to be rich soon?), and frustration (only if I didn't miss the breakout or did this or did that ...).

As much as we know that we should not to chase a stock if we missed the breakout or we are out of position, we will still chase sometimes. And I don't think we learn until we have chased and suffered financially and mentally. I'm sure there are a few traders out there who have never chased a trade. But chances are we are not one of them. I certainly was not.

Gamestop Corp.

Let's examine another tricky breakout:

FIGURE 83

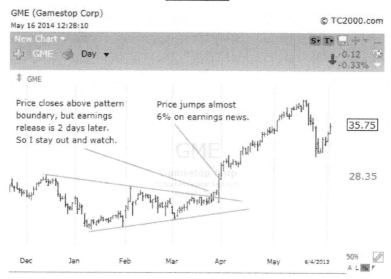

GME (Gamestop Corp)
May 16 2014 12:28:10

© TC2000.com

New Chart ▾

GME   Day ▾

-0.12
-0.33%

GME

Price closes above pattern
boundary, but earnings
release is 2 days later.
So I stay out and watch.

Price jumps almost
6% on earnings news.

35.75

28.35

Dec   Jan   Feb   Mar   Apr   May   6/4/2013

50%

Gamestop Corp. formed a well-defined 3-month symmetrical triangle from December 2012 to March 2013. On March 26, the stock closed above the upper boundary. But I would not have bought shares because the next quarterly earnings report was to be released two days later. I would wait and see where prices settle after the earnings report. The stock jumped 6% on earnings news.

How should we trade this breakout? Should we trade it at all?

Buying shares around the closing price of the 6% day would mean entering at a spot where the reward-to-risk ratio is unfavorable. We would be risking about 8% of our position if we were to use the last day rule to place our stop-loss order. Only in hindsight do we know that there was no difficult retest and the stock gained more than 100% in the next six months. The decisive breakout could have failed decisively and produced a quick 8% loss on our position.

If we were to enter this trade after the 6% jump, I think we should buy a smaller-than-normal position so that an 8% loss (remember that it is always possible that we lose more if there is a downward price gap) on our position still keeps our loss to less than 1% of our total capital. Even if we use a smaller position, we are still chasing. And when I chase, my rule is to not attempt another trade if I get stopped out. I have found that chasing, even with a smaller position, always creates negative emotions. I get anxious about the trade rather than staying detached and doing other things. Anxiety throws off our mental game and increases the likelihood that we will do the wrong things, such as not honoring our stops or chasing again and entering at increasingly unfavorable and riskier spots.

So, we should do our best not to chase. If we chase, we should do so with a small position. And we must move on if we are stopped out.

ShoreTel, Inc.

Here's another breakout that, depending on our risk tolerance and trading style, may have been untradeable:

FIGURE 84

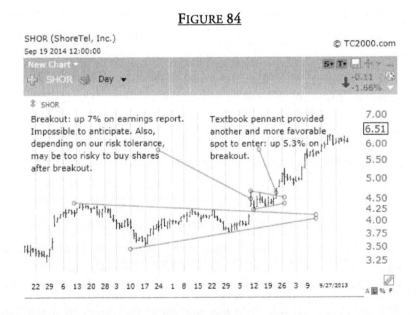

We have a textbook symmetrical triangle with a decisive breakout on the day of the quarterly earnings release. The breakout was strong: up more than 7% on the day. Entering around the closing price of the breakout day meant risking more than 7% of our position. If we had bought shares earlier during the breakout day when prices were higher, we were risking more than 10%. If we did not want to risk around 10% of a normal-size or even smaller position, then we could wait and observe. **Doing nothing is always an option.** A quick and focused glance once a day would inform us of new chart developments that may create a more favorable entry spot.

The next day, we saw a retest that dropped the stock 2.2%. If we chose to buy shares now, we would be risking less than 5% rather than more than 7% of our position, a big difference. Let's say we decided to wait for an even more favorable entry spot. Or, we may have simply missed this decline. Perhaps there would be a hard retest that drops prices all the way down to the upper boundary of the symmetrical triangle. There was no hard retest, but instead of being disappointed, we would be wise to continue to monitor the chart. And our diligence would alert us to a possible 2-week continuation pennant developing just above the pattern boundary. A decisive breakout from this pennant gave us another chance to buy shares while risking just over 5% of our position.

In addition to providing a more favorable reward-to-risk possibility than the initial breakout, this pennant had another favorable attribute: greater likelihood of producing an immediate follow through. I have found that breakouts from small pennants and flags have a high success rate. I would buy shares on the day of the breakout from the pennant and set my stop using the last day rule. If the breakout was to reverse and the pennant fail, then I would simply move on. I have found that it is easier to move on after getting stopped out of a position I entered at an advantageous spot compared to after getting stopped out from chasing an unfavorable trade. Why? I think there is a significant satisfaction knowing that I lost a very manageable amount of my capital to make a bet with a favorable reward-to-risk possibility. It is about trading correctly regardless of the outcome. If a promising pennant fails, I accept it, and I think about how I focused on doing the right things, such as waiting for a more favorable entry spot. **Trading well is so much about our mental state. A losing trade can increase our confidence if we know that we traded the set-up well.** We look forward to applying our knowledge and exercising our discipline on the next promising set-up. We know that have no control over whether our next trade will be profitable. But we also know that we have full control over how we trade and that if we trade correctly then even a losing streak will keep our losses small.

CHAPTER 26
Taking Profits

So far we have focused, with very good reason, on how to enter trades at favorable spots and how to place stop-loss orders to limit possible losses. We can make money only if we have money to bet on promising set-ups. Preserving our trading capital requires strict money management. It is far better to miss a breakout and not make money than to chase and lose money. Focusing on limiting losses is proper and productive.

Once we understand the foundational importance of protecting our trading capital, we also need to learn how to take profits. We discussed how to estimate the possible price target of a pattern breakout by projecting up or down the height of the pattern at its widest from the point of breakout. This projection is called the measured price target. It is only a general guideline. Breakouts can reverse and fail any time. Or a pattern breakout may fail to reach the measured price target even though it made a strong run and produced a significant profit. Or prices may continue to surge higher or lower well past the price targets. We should not be disappointed in the lack of certainty. Looking for guarantees in the financial markets is asking for confusion, frustration, and pain.

Instead, we can use the very unscientific nature of the measured price target "rule" to help manage risk and make money. I almost always take profits on my entire position if a price target is hit. Also, I often take profits on part of my position if a breakout has reached the halfway mark to the price target. Sometimes I will do so with the intention of adding to my position if there is a retest and prices return to the pattern boundary. Because patterns can fail anytime, I don't mind erring on the side of having taken profits "too soon." I tend to take profits when there are profits to be taken, especially at or around the price target.

That said, I don't think we should exit a position the moment it is sitting on a profit. Ironically, taking profits too quickly can lead to a destructive cycle.

If we seem to be exiting many positions with only a tiny profit, then we are likely watching our screens too much. We are watching nervously every price tick and getting scared every time the price action is unfavorable. We cannot trade well and do the right things with such an anxious state of mind. We will be mentally exhausted and lacking discipline, which lead to large losses.

If we have done our homework, identified a promising breakout, and entered at a favorable spot with a very manageable possible loss, we should give our position time to work (make significant progress toward the price target) or fail (trigger our stop). If we are unable to let go after entering a trade, if we cannot stand taking even a small loss, then we must not trade stocks or any financial instrument. There is absolutely nothing wrong with deciding that we have no interest in trading. We all have different interests, personalities, and aptitudes. And we don't have to prove anything to anyone, especially in the markets. **If we are not willing to take many small losses as the regular and expected part of trading, then we are almost guaranteed to suffer large losses**. Let's see how this disaster can happen.

Say that we bought shares after a strong breakout. We are sitting on a nice profit as prices surge higher. Then prices reverse and our profits have almost entirely disappeared. We think about exiting with a small gain but we "want to make back our profits that we had only days ago." But prices continue to decline and we are now sitting on a loss. A small loss, but we are annoyed. We "want our money back." So we wait and stay in our position even when prices continue to decline and reach our stop-loss level. Instead of allowing our stop-loss order to take us out of our position for a still minor loss, we cancel our stop-loss order and stay in. Prices are now crashing. We still don't get out because we want to get out when we are respectably close to breaking even. The stock continues to decline and our losses grow. We eventually exit with a huge loss.

And things don't necessarily get better. We are embarrassed. And angry. The market owes us. So we trade ill-defined patterns and poor set-ups. We continue to lose money. We are now on what can only be called the **cycle of pain and greed**. There is a way off this satanic treadmill. Exit our positions, step away from our screen, and take a break for several days or even weeks. Muster the courage to think about why we made these mistakes. Reflect on how we can improve. Affirm that we can do better. Realize that there will always be more opportunities. Calm down. Forgive ourselves. Focus on doing the right things. Return to the basics.

Too dramatic? Unfortunately, no. I think all of us will (must?) take at least one ride on this treadmill of pain. It seems sometimes experiencing pain is the only way we learn.

To avoid this destructive cycle, I try to stay in a trade until it is resolved either by prices hitting or having made significant progress to the price target or getting stopped out. Meanwhile, I try to ignore my positions and stay away from the screens as much as possible during market hours. I remind myself that I am bigger than my positions. We are bigger than the small losses we will take. We are also bigger than the large profits we could make. As in life, self-respect is necessary before success in trading.

Mechel Steel Group

Mechel Steel formed a textbook ascending triangle from June to September 2013:

FIGURE 85

The breakout was decisive and the follow through immediate. The price target was hit two days after the breakout. At this point, I would have taken profits on at least two-thirds of my position. Why not sell the entire position? I should, and I usually do. But there is always the temptation to keep my position to make more money if the uptrend continues. Also, the breakout and price target were achieved in three days while the ascending triangle formed for three months. There is something unsatisfactory about diligently tracking a pattern for months and even years and then see the price target reached in less than a week. We want more. We want to ride the money train for at least several weeks. In addition, a continuation pattern might form after the price target is hit so we'll just stay with our position instead of risk missing a fast breakout from a pennant or flag.

But there are also good reasons to exit once the price target is hit. The measured price target is just a possibility, and prices could have stopped well short of the target. Also, an immediate follow through after a breakout is a good thing as we don't have to deal with retests. This 3-day trek to the price target may not seem like much of a move on the chart but that is an almost 18% gain. It is a big gain in such a short time and it will build our capital. Finally, we gain confidence in our ability to trade while managing risk.

So what to do when the price target is hit? I see three options.

First, get out completely and move on.

Second, take profits on most of our position and let the remainder ride. If the stock continues to surge then fine but we won't add to our position unless there is a compelling continuation pattern that provides an advantageous entry spot. If prices reverse and we get stopped out on the position we kept, then that's it and we move on.

Third, keep our entire position even when the price target is hit. But we're done if we get stopped out at our original stop-loss level.

I almost always choose the first or second option and I think most of us should as well. If we choose the third option and get stopped out after prices reverse, then we have to remember that we had prepared for this loss. Try not to think of the evaporated profits as money we lost. Instead, focus on having entered at a favorable spot and consider taking profits earlier next time.

Here, selling our shares at the price target turned out well. Of course we had no way of knowing the optimal strategy. The stock paused after hitting the price target and traded in a narrow range for 7 days. It was reasonable to think that a possible continuation pennant or flag was forming. But instead of a fast uptrend out of a pennant or flag, prices dropped to the upper boundary of the ascending triangle.

Some scenarios to consider:

If we sold our position at the price target or missed the breakout, then it was worth considering whether we should buy a position when prices returned to the upper boundary. I do not usually re-enter a position on a chart where prices have hit the measured target and then returned to the breakout level. My reasoning is that the chart pattern that launched the successful move has served its purpose. But support and resistance levels are often enduring. The upper boundary of the ascending triangle was resistance prior to breakout and it may now be effective support. So we may decide to buy a position just above the upper boundary of the ascending triangle with a relatively tight stop. If we get stopped out, then we move on. If the boundary holds up against retests and pushes prices back up, then fine.

As we see in Figure 85, the upper boundary held as support over four days of retests. But the stock closed below the upper boundary on the fifth day and then decisively closed deep inside the pattern over the next several days. If we had bought shares during the retests, we were stopped out with a small loss. At this point, for a while at least, I was no longer interested in trading this chart. The ascending triangle had served its purpose by hitting its price target and then also became invalid when the upper boundary failed as a support level. There was no tradable classical pattern on the chart. Of course Mechel Steel's chart will continue to evolve and perhaps form another tradable classical pattern, but that possibility was probably months away.

Let's discuss another scenario from this chart. Let's say we held on to our position even when the price target was met. We were counting on a continuation flag or pennant forming and riding another powerful uptrend. Instead, prices declined to the upper boundary. We were disappointed when our profits disappeared but we hoped for the upper boundary to hold as support and push prices up. Then we were stopped out when the upper boundary failed to hold as support. What we must do now is move on knowing that we took a reasonable risk by not selling at the price target and counting on a continuation flag or pennant to develop. We must also remember that we lost only a very small slice of our trading account. Indeed, we expected to lose this modest sum when we entered this trade and set our stop. Again, we must not count the profits that disappeared as a loss. But what is absolutely the worst thing we can do is to re-enter this trade to get our money back. By early October, this chart is "broken." There is simply no tradable pattern. In mid-November, the stock dropped 30% in one day before closing the day down 23%.

The overall lesson is that we must accept the fact that there is no trading method that maximizes our profit in all situations. The wise decision is to adopt a strategy that manages our risk in all market conditions. It means sometimes selling at the price target and then watching the stock explode higher. It means sometimes watching prices trigger our stop and then immediately turn around and take off without us. We must accept these disappointments with maturity and calm because we understand that protecting our capital, not making money, is our priority.

CHAPTER 27
Why We Must Diversify Our Trades

As we gain experience and have some winning trades, we can get overconfident and forget that the reason we are finding success is because we have been focused on the fundamentals, namely, limiting losses and managing risk. Overconfidence can lead to taking a large position in a single stock. Why go for only steady gains when we can make a lot on one trade? The following chart shows why we must always diversify our trades, especially when things are going well and we are most vulnerable to overconfidence, and never bet it all on a single position:

FIGURE 86

In July 2013, NQ Mobile broke out of a giant descending flag or channel that had been forming for over four months. Prices nearly tripled over the next three months. The breakout and follow through were so strong that the stock had only a couple of down days during the month following the breakout. If we had taken profits on two-thirds of our position in, say, late July or early August, and decided to hold onto the rest, we saw NQ Mobile form a textbook uptrend channel from August to October 2013 that continued to push prices higher. We are human, so we may regret getting out "so early" instead of focusing on how we kept a portion of our original position. At this point, there is one thing that we must not do: buy more shares, and, driven by the frustration over selling earlier, perhaps go all in on this stock. We should not dismiss this possibility. We are very capable of buying shares at the September or October highs even though there was no tradable pattern with an advantageous entry spot. The only classical trading principle that could guide us in September and October was the rising channel, but it, like all patterns, had multiple possible interpretations. A bullish rising channel could just as easily be seen as a bearish giant rising flag. Whatever our interpretation, our overall conclusion should have been that there was no favorable entry spot with a compelling reward-to-risk possibility. Therefore, I don't think we had a compelling reason to add to our position or start a new position at these price levels. If anything, we should have been considering selling our remaining position.

Then in late October, the stock dropped 47% in one day. Even this disaster did not hurt us if we took partial profits in July or August and did not recklessly add to our remaining position or initiate a new position in August, September, or October. If we took profits, we still earned a small or even significant profit. But if we chased and bought shares anytime from August to October, then we lost nearly half of our position or account if we went all in.

This crash was unrelated to an earnings report. And the cause does not matter because such unpredictable events can happen anytime to any stock. We simply have no control over unexpected news that crashes a stock. We can control how much we bet on a stock. I usually commit at most no more than 7-8% of my account to a single position. By always diversifying our trades and entering only when there is a compelling opportunity, we can reduce our risk to very manageable levels and survive even market crashes.

One more thing about the August to October price action. Some people will prefer to interpret it as a powerful uptrend within a well-defined rising channel. Others will like to see it as a giant bearish flag. As we discussed, it is fine to have an opinion but we must be mentally flexible and honest enough to at least recognize that there is an alternative interpretation. If we only saw a powerful uptrend within a textbook rising channel and ignored all contrary interpretations, then we were closing our eyes to risk, and such willful blindness is always costly. If we preferred the bullish rising channel view and bought shares toward the lower boundary of the channel, but we also recognized the opposite and potentially dangerous bearish rising flag possibility, then we were much more likely to use an appropriate position size that would have reduced our losses to a manageable amount.

CHAPTER 28

The Trader's Routine: Continuous Patience and Diligence

Winners have systems.

Scott Adams

We need not, indeed, must not, spend 13 hours a day staring at charts. However, we must be diligent in doing our homework by regularly monitoring our charts. A quick, focused, and efficient glance at a chart every several days to every couple of weeks will allow us to identify, monitor, and trade many interesting classical patterns. Some exceptions are the fast-forming and fast-moving small flags and pennants that can last as few as three days or so. But since many flags and pennants form after breaking out of much larger patterns that are easier to spot and track, we can create a list of stocks that justify more frequent, such as daily, check-ins. We cannot and should not try to catch and trade every classical pattern that forms in the markets. Several promising patterns are enough.

Since most patterns take many weeks and months to form, I would describe the skill and attitude needed to be a good trader as one of long-term patience and diligence. Let's say we have about 700 to 800 stocks on our watch list and we usually take about a week or two to review them. If we spot an interesting chart, we can save it in one of several folders categorized by the urgency of the set-up. For example, we can have a folder for charts that have already formed an identifiable classical pattern and may

245

be close to a breakout. Another folder can be for patterns where the breakout does not seem imminent. Yet another folder can be for set-ups that may be in the process of forming a classical pattern but no clear pattern can be identified yet. And another folder can be for charts that have potential, such as those that show clear resistance and support levels. So we can cycle through our stock list about every two weeks while checking in on our urgent folders more regularly and perhaps even daily.

Let's see how this trading process might work in real life using the following set-ups.

Matrix Service Co.

FIGURE 87

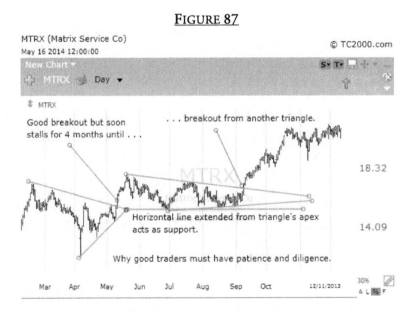

It is late February 2013. We start to go through our stock list and see nothing interesting about the chart of Matrix Service Co.

We cycle through our list over two weeks and come back to Matrix Service in mid-March. Again, nothing noteworthy. We come back to it in early April and still don't see any identifiable classical pattern.

But by late April it seems that prices are coiling and forming a possible symmetrical triangle. We put this chart in one of our more urgent folders and review it every day.

There is a decisive breakout in early May and a strong follow through into mid-May. Let's say we bought shares around the closing price of the breakout day and set our stop-loss order just below the low. We are happy about the strong follow through but we try not to get too excited and instead we move on and continue to cycle through our stock list. Two weeks later in early June we see that the stock has declined from the May highs. We consider this decline normal as no stock goes straight up and we know that we have to expect retests. Another two weeks later, in the middle of June, prices are essentially unchanged.

But there are somewhat disappointing developments when we come back to the chart in late June. The stock has dropped further and is now trading at about the level where we would have placed our stop-loss order. If our stop-loss order was triggered, then we were out with a small loss. No big deal. There was nothing to get angry about. Small losses are part of trading. At this point, we had no urgent interest in this chart. But that did not mean we would ignore this chart forever. We would review this chart every couple of weeks as part of our regular search for trade set-ups.

In mid-July, we saw that the stock had bounced up nicely from the lows of late June. But, and this point is crucial, we do nothing because there was nothing to do: we did not see a tradable classical pattern with a compelling entry opportunity. So we continue to cycle through our stock list. In early August we saw that this stock was trading in a range and was perhaps forming a descending triangle since the highs of mid-May. We put this stock in our folder for medium-urgency set-ups and check in every several days or so. By mid-August a descending triangle did seem to be forming and an imminent downward breakout seemed possible. We move this chart into our folder for the most urgent set-ups and check it daily. Still, we must not get fixated on a single possibility and instead we must keep our minds open and flexible. We know that patterns can fail and evolve into a very different look.

It is now late August. It is still possible that a descending triangle in forming. But we see another, perhaps more compelling, possibility: a symmetrical triangle. The strongest clue that a symmetrical rather than a descending triangle was forming was the rising lower boundary of a possible symmetrical triangle. This rising lower boundary was not evident in the middle of August but had six or seven solid price touches by late August and even more by early September. Since symmetrical triangles can break up or down, we continue to stay mentally nimble. We check the chart daily and catch the breakout a few days later. We decide to buy shares around the closing price of the breakout day and set our stop just below the low. Then we move on and continue our routine of cycling through our stock list while also checking more frequently our more urgent set-ups.

This multi-month routine we described is the ideal, but it is still a reasonable and reachable goal for us. It is within our power to do everything that was described.

Let's discuss an interesting event from this pattern. When prices declined to the breakout level in late June, did the pattern fail? I say no. It is true that prices returned to the breakout level without reaching the measured price target. But, again, the target is only a possibility and the breakout did launch a significant uptrend. And prices could still reach the price target.

Was there are any reason to expect the late-June lows to hold and possibly reverse the downtrend? Notice how if we extend a horizontal line from the apex of the triangle (the pointed end), that level held as support during the late-June lows. Prices briefly traded a bit below the apex level but did not close below it. Edwards & Magee wrote more than 50 years ago that the apex level of a symmetrical triangle can be a support level. Here, this principle worked as the apex level supported prices for the next two months and was the basis of a textbook and powerful symmetrical triangle.

Should we trade bounces off of apex-based support? I will consider trading any pattern or situation that has a clearly defined and favorable reward-to-risk scenario. For example, here I can buy shares around the apex support level and place my stop just below a recent low. I am risking a fraction of a percent of my position on a clearly-defined situation: I can make significant gains if support holds and prices go up while I will lose a small fraction of my position if support fails (barring a big downward price gap). As with any trade, a favorable entry spot is key. If an apex level serves as powerful support and quickly reverses a downtrend, then the bounce off support may be so strong as to force me to chase the rebound and enter at a spot where I must risk more than prudent.

Lastly, let's return to the topic of this chapter, and, really this book: patience and diligence. Almost two months passed from the breakout from the first symmetrical triangle to the retest of the apex-level support in late June. And it was another 10 weeks until the breakout from the second symmetrical triangle. We needed discipline to regularly check the chart to spot important developments. We needed patience to give the pattern time to evolve knowing that there was no guarantee that the chart would form a tradable pattern despite our vigilance over many months. There are also the inevitable boredom and anxiety associated with such permanent uncertainty. Only in hindsight does it seem "obvious" that a symmetrical triangle was forming. Only now does it seem like it was easy to wait the almost four months it took for the second symmetrical triangle to form. We must not think that ideal set-ups will present themselves to us whenever we feel like looking at some charts. Taking advantage of compelling set-ups requires following a regular and diligent routine over many months, and the process must never stop if we are to trade well over the long run.

In short, I think it is impossible to be a successful classical chartist over the long-run without being substantially at peace with ourselves before we start to trade. We simply will not have the patience, composure, and calm to diligently apply a systematic trading process over many weeks, months, and years if we are looking for personal validation and quick riches in the markets. I don't mean that being at peace will spare us from a steep and challenging learning curve. I am saying we will be much more likely to survive the difficult trading periods that we will experience if we commit ourselves to being grateful and reflective regardless of our trading results.

Ryland Group

Our next chart is another example of the necessity and rewards of diligently applying a systematic trading process over months and years:

FIGURE 88

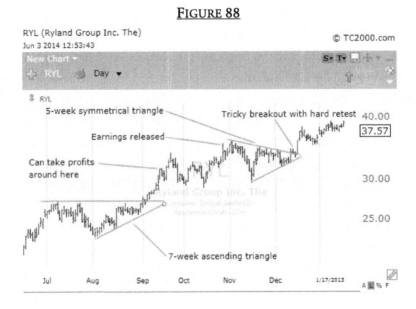

In early July, we did not see anything interesting on Ryland Group's chart. So we move on. A few weeks later, we see something noteworthy. In late July, we see prices were turned back right around a high established several weeks ago. We draw a horizontal line just above the two peaks to signify a possibly significant resistance level. If this level does turn out to be an important resistance, then a breakout through this zone will be important and perhaps a trading opportunity. For now, we do not see a classical pattern so we just wait for further chart development. But we know that patterns can form quickly and how seemingly meaningless price action can be the beginning of a textbook pattern, so we put this chart in our medium-urgency folder for more frequent check-ins, say, every 3 to 4 days vs. every 7-to-10 days.

Two more weeks pass and it is early August, and we don't see anything interesting. But there is something interesting in another two weeks. Our preliminary horizontal line indicating a possible resistance level has again turned back prices. Two touches can be just coincidence, but three or more touches on a potential pattern boundary are noteworthy. And there was another development: a possible rising lower boundary with 4 or 5 touches. We now put this chart in our urgent folder for daily review. If an ascending triangle was forming and if the lower boundary had already been established, then a breakout could happen soon. But everything is only a possibility before the pattern completion and breakout. Prices could plunge below our preliminary lower boundary and the chart could continue to evolve for weeks or months into nothing. We will check the chart daily but we will not do anything unless there is an actionable development that provides a compelling trade.

On the last day of trading in August, the stock made a strong upward move and closed just under the upper boundary of this potential ascending triangle. A breakout could be imminent. Or the chart could continue to evolve for a while. So we watch rather than jump in. The next day stock broke through and closed decisively above the upper boundary. The stock was up 2.35% on the day so buying around the closing price and setting a stop just below the breakout day low meant risking a very reasonable amount of our position for a promising pattern and breakout. Then we immediately face a challenge. The following day prices decline by 1.24% and, perhaps more ominously, close slightly below the upper boundary.

Should we sell our position? Were we tricked by the "breakout" that was in fact a nasty bull trap or just an insignificant out-of-line price movement? It was possible that the breakout was a false move. It was also possible that the 1.24% decline was a normal hard retest. Nobody could know. My opinion is that we should stay in our position until there is a resolution to the trade. If prices continued to decline, then we were stopped out for a minor loss and we move on to other set-ups. If the 1.24% decline turns out to be a normal retest after which prices increase, then fine.

Such composure is our goal. It is not that we should not care. That is impossible. We should care. We should take great care to enter only at compelling spots. But we have no control over prices. Obsessing after we enter only causes anxiety and can undo the patient work we did to identify and enter a compelling set-up. If we did our homework before entering a trade, then we have to learn to let go. Since we will use strict money management and risk only a fraction of our trading account on any single trade, we are not bothered too much about the prospect of getting stopped out. We can stay detached and give the pattern time to work.

Here, we did our homework before entering and bought shares after a clear breakout that provided a compelling entry spot. We did all we can and thus we do not obsess over the outcome. Several days later we saw that the pattern survived the hard retest and launched a strong follow through that reached the price target. We sell our shares for a nice profit at the measured price target. And for now, we move on from this chart. We will review the chart as part of our regular cycling through of our stock list rather than checking it daily. We don't see any compelling set-ups on this chart for the next two months.

We know that continuous patience and diligence are necessary to identify promising patterns so we continue to review the chart every couple of weeks or so. By late November we see a descending resistance line that could possibly form the boundary of a tradable pattern. We put this chart in our folder for more frequent reviews and check in every several days. By early December we see an ascending support line that could be the lower boundary of a possible symmetrical triangle. Now we move this chart into our urgent folder for daily review to maximize our chances of catching a potential breakout. Several days later prices break out of the 5-week symmetrical triangle. After a hard retest, prices moved quickly up.

We will never know when or whether the charts we are monitoring will produce a tradable pattern. But the only way we will spot compelling setups and decisive breakouts is to always do our homework by cycling through our stock list, drawing and redrawing possible boundaries, and staying patient. There is no other way. If we are beginners and just started to look at charts, we may not find a tradable pattern for weeks or even months. The market is not required to give us a welcome basket full of compelling chart set-ups just because we decided to trade. We have to be patient. We must not be so eager to trade and make money that we waste our capital by trading weak set-ups and non-patterns.

Lastly, a five-week symmetrical triangle is a relatively small pattern. It was easy to miss this pattern even if we examined the price action daily in late November. Many patterns are much easier to spot when framed by boundaries. Therefore, we should always tirelessly draw and redraw preliminary pattern boundaries for an evolving chart. **Boundaries frame and focus our view and help us spot and track meaningful price developments.**

Xerium Technologies

Our next chart is a great example of the rewards of patience and how turning our attention elsewhere after entering a trade is often the best and only thing we can do:

FIGURE 89

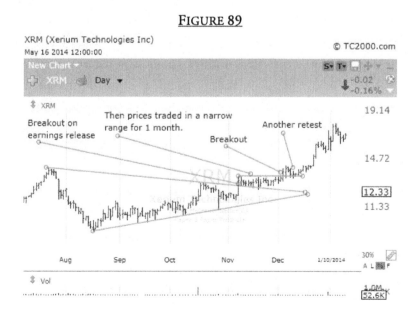

253

A 14-week symmetrical triangle. We did not see anything resembling a classical pattern from July to early September. Only by late September did we see a rising support level from the mid-August low. With four solid touches, this ascending boundary was potentially significant and thus we put this chart in our folder for set-ups requiring more frequent review. In early October, we saw that the rising support line successfully supported two more price touches. We continue to check in every several days and stay patient. In late October, we see that the rising support line has earned another price touch and that a possible upper boundary of a potential symmetrical triangle has been established. The pattern seems to be maturing so we check it daily. **We should always find out as soon as possible the release date of the next quarterly earnings report**. We find that Xerium Technologies is due to release its earnings report in about a week, in early November. We wait and watch. Prices decisively break out from the symmetrical triangle on earnings news. The breakout is powerful: up 8.78% for the day.

Given this powerful breakout, we can decide to buy a smaller position. Another and more important reason is that Xerium is a very thin stock. All stocks are subject to fast moves and large price gaps, but very low-volume stocks are more vulnerable. In fact, we should generally avoid trading such low-volume stocks unless we do so with a significantly reduced position and only if there is a compelling reason to trade. Here, the breakout was decisive and on heavy volume and closed above a significant prior high. That said, risk management, not making money, must be our focus and priority so we should use a much smaller position or avoid trading this kind of set-up.

We decide to buy a small position, set our stop just below the low of the breakout day, and move on. We have done all we can for this chart. We continue to cycle through our stock list to spot promising set-ups on other charts. While such detachment is easier said than done, it must be our goal if we are to achieve long-term success. We do our homework before we enter a trade. Afterwards, we should be indifferent toward our positions.

A carefree attitude focused on other tasks after entering a position will always be beneficial, as it was here. After breaking out, prices traded in a narrow range just above the pattern boundary for a month. Also, there were two hard retests that traded below the upper boundary of the symmetrical triangle. Prices broke above the trading range a month after breakout. Then prices traded in another narrow range for two weeks before starting a sustained uptrend. So prices essentially went nowhere for six weeks after a decisive breakout. If we had watched every price tick or even if we checked the post-breakout progress only every day or so, we were almost certain to lose patience and sell our position.

As we discussed, there are reasonable arguments against waiting six weeks for a breakout to reach a resolution. Here, only in hindsight do we know that a powerful uptrend started six weeks after breakout. Some traders look for trades to work almost immediately in their favor. Otherwise, even if their position is sitting on a small profit, they will exit their position and move on because their valuable capital and time can be deployed in other set-ups. Others give more time for a pattern to work.

I think there are reasonable arguments in favor of moving on after a couple of weeks of waiting. We should consider these arguments and adopt them if they fit our personality and trading style. But even if we decide to give our trades less leeway, we still must avoid following too closely the price action after we enter trades because micromanaging trades is the path to a destructive negative feedback loop. Micromanagement is so bad precisely because it sometimes works and rewards us for our bad behavior.

For example, let's say that we bought a position in Xerium Technologies after the breakout. We anxiously watch the post-breakout action as prices, rather than surging up, are hugging the upper boundary of the symmetrical triangle. When there is a hard retest in mid-November, we have had enough. We sell our shares. Then let's assume that prices, instead of eventually surging upwards in mid-December, continued to decline and that the pattern failed. We were feeling brilliant instead of merely lucky for "anticipating" the pattern failure. We tell ourselves that we knew the pattern was bound to fail. Besides humorous and dangerous self-deception, what have we gained? True, we saved a bit of money by selling at a higher price than we would have had our stop-loss order been triggered at the lower price. But because our position size was appropriate to begin with, selling at the stop-loss price would still have meant a very small loss. The only "reward" was that we were rewarded for our bad trading behavior.

In fact, the money we "saved" is inconsequential compared to what we have lost. **We spent our most valuable possessions, time and energy, obsessing about the price action, which we have zero control over**. Why do we act as if prices will obey our wishes if we watch them closely? Having spent our energy on a futile task, we are more tired than we need to be. And fatigue makes it much more likely that we will trade badly and make mistakes. Fatigue means more anxiety and less patience. We find it difficult to stay patient and calm. Instead, we are prone to chasing breakouts and entering where there is no compelling trade. Worse, what if, instead of the pattern failing as in our hypothetical, we sold our position a week before prices finally surged upwards? We might kick ourselves for being so impatient. So we chase the breakout, perhaps with a too-big position. When prices inevitably pause and decline, we get stopped out for a large loss. We are angry and anxious to make back our money the market "owes" us. So we chase again and again with larger positions and the losses mount. It is the familiar cycle of great pain and frustration.

The way to avoid this negative loop is simple: we must be bigger than our trading results. And we are. Stop obsessing over a trade and let go. Be like Han Solo: cool, calm, and nonchalant. The foundation of such detachment is risk management: trading only compelling set-ups and risking only a fraction of our trading account on any given trade, we are indifferent to the outcome.

TRW Automotive Holdings

Our next set-up emphasizes again the need for and the benefits of sustained diligence.

First, the weekly chart:

FIGURE 90

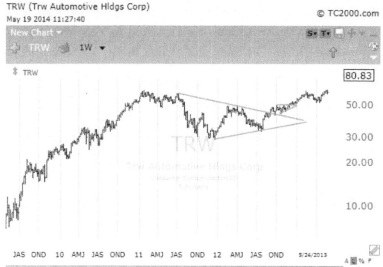

A 14-month symmetrical triangle formed after a 2-year rally from the 2009 lows. Before we examine the daily chart, let's talk about any biases we may have had with this set-up. I'll tell you what my bias was. I thought surely this possible symmetrical triangle will be a reversal pattern. I had a difficult time accepting even the possibility that the stock could continue to go up after rising 43-fold from March 2009 to March 2011.

But, of course, prices could continue to go up. There is something irresistible about picking the tops and bottoms of a price move. With TRW having risen so much over several years, we liked the idea of shorting shares at possibly the very end of a multi-year uptrend. We missed the gigantic uptrend from the depths of the 2007-2009 financial crisis, but we sure won't miss the crash from the top. This is exactly the wrong mindset. If we are so focused on a particular result, then we will fight the trend and lose money and miss a profitable trade. We must continuously fight our biases and wishes to keep our eyes open and accept the actual price action.

Let's return to analyzing the chart of TRW. We saw nothing resembling a classical pattern during the first year of the construction of this symmetrical triangle. Only by continuously checking the chart as part of our regular browsing process, and also by occasionally checking the weekly chart to get a big-picture view of the price action, could we spot this pattern. And despite the pattern's large size and well-formed shape, it was not easy to spot it. Part of the reason is that the six significant highs and lows that touch the upper and lower boundaries are spread over 14 months. **Again, constantly drawing and redrawing preliminary pattern boundaries made spotting and tracking the pattern much easier because boundaries frame and focus our view of the price action.** They also alert us to the need to redraw our preliminary lines when prices overshoot them. And they also confirm the significance of a boundary by staying within them.

Now let's focus on the breakout using a daily chart:

FIGURE 90.1

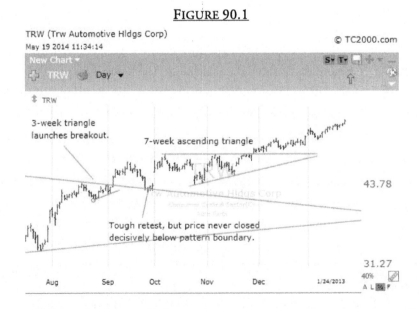

By early August 2013, we saw that a possible significant low had been established in late July and that this possible symmetrical triangle now had at least four solid touches framing it. As a continuation symmetrical triangle can launch a breakout after four touches, we know that a possible breakout could happen soon. So we put this chart in one of our more urgent folders for more frequent check-ins. In mid-August, prices touched the upper boundary but was turned back. This price action was significant because it was the fourth touch on the upper boundary and it also supported the interpretation that our upper boundary was a meaningful boundary and resistance. Perhaps prices would make another attempt at overcoming and closing above the upper boundary. Or, prices could fail to break above the upper boundary and instead drop through the lower boundary and complete a reversal symmetrical triangle. Or the chart could evolve into something entirely different. These are all possibilities that we have to be open to while we wait for a compelling reason to enter this set-up.

By late August and early September, we saw a possible 3-week symmetrical triangle forming just under the upper boundary. This small pattern had the potential to launch a powerful upward breakout or a downtrend. The situation was resolved when prices decisively shot up from the small triangle and the larger 14-month triangle on September 6. Prices went up 4.5% on the breakout day and so we could enter around the closing price and set our stop just below the day's low. Prices moved higher for a week before pausing and reversing for a hard retest where prices traded below the upper boundary. Depending on where we placed out stop-loss order, this hard retest could have triggered our stop.

Let's say we were stopped out and disappointed, but we continued to focus and evaluate the chart. We thought it was significant that during the retest prices traded but did not close below the boundary. This fact, combined with the initial decisive breakout from a significant pattern, suggested that we should continue to monitor this set-up.

In fact, some of us may decide to re-enter very soon after being stopped out. We could enter around the closing price of the hard retest day and set our stop just below the low. The rationale for this second trade is that the upper pattern boundary kept prices from closing below it and thus the pattern and breakout were still valid. We also had a clearly defined and, in my opinion, favorable reward-to-risk scenario. If the retest was over, then prices would rebound. If prices continued to decline, then we got stopped out for a likely 1.4% loss on our second entry.

If we saw no compelling reason to re-enter so soon after the hard retest, then we could wait and continue to monitor the chart. We saw prices jump almost 8% three days after the hard retest. Did we make a mistake by staying out? No. Waiting for a more compelling entry spot was a reasonable decision. Most importantly, we absolutely must not chase. If prices had continued to streak up after the 8% jump, then we have to accept it and let it go. Let it go. We did not do anything wrong. And, let's say it together: there will always be other and more compelling set-ups to trade.

As it happened, prices stalled again at around the previous significant high and generally declined as the next quarterly earnings report approached. If we had bought shares after the hard retest, then we should sell our shares. If we had not re-entered this trade after getting stopped out, then we would wait until the earnings report is released and see how the chart looks afterwards. The earnings announcement in late October caused prices to rise modestly but there was no reason to buy shares. There was no continuation pattern that presented a good entry spot.

So far we had the initial breakout from the giant symmetrical triangle, which was tradable, a hard retest, which likely stopped us out and could be seen as a relatively attractive re-entry point, and range-bound trading before and after the earnings report. Since we now had no compelling pattern to trade, we would wait and continue to watch the chart.

One thing we noticed was that the post-earnings rise in early November was turned back at exactly the prior high reached in early October. We had a potentially significant resistance level that could form the boundary of a classical pattern yet to be formed. Prices declined into mid-November before reversing and going up. Prices turned up just above a preliminary rising support boundary we had drawn and therefore we conclude that an ascending triangle was possibly forming. We check daily the chart and see prices breaking out decisively from the ascending triangle in late November. Now we had a clear breakout from a textbook classical pattern and a compelling reason to enter a trade at a spot with a favorable reward-to-risk ratio.

What were the key ingredients to spotting and trading this entry signal? Consistent patience and diligence. The breakout from the 7-week continuation ascending triangle came almost three months after the initial and exciting breakout from the 14-month symmetrical triangle. When the initial breakout fizzled and stopped us out, we were disappointed and inclined to forget this chart and move on. And it is important not to dwell pointlessly on why there was no powerful and immediate follow through. But an even better approach is to have the courage, patience, and diligence to periodically check back to see if the chart was evolving to form another trade opportunity. Why courage? We all get discouraged, especially when a promising set-up does not work in our favor. Our natural inclination is to trash the chart and never look at it again. Instead, we could periodically glance at the chart to spot interesting price action.

Trading well is never about forcing meaning onto a chart. We can never make things happen by being anxious and impatient. We can only participate in price moves launched by classical patterns. And we need continuous diligence and patience to spot compelling set-ups.

General Dynamics

Let's finish this chapter with one of my favorite charts from the past couple of years. Here is a weekly chart of a 27-month symmetrical triangle:

FIGURE 91

A perfect giant symmetrical triangle. It is tempting to think that all we had to do to make money was buy shares at the breakout. But remember that we are looking at this pattern in hindsight. Trading in real time is challenging, even with a giant pattern staring at us.

What was required to trade this set-up well? Again, we needed patience and diligence to spot, track, and trade this symmetrical triangle. Of course we would not look daily at this chart for twenty-seven months. There was nothing to make sense of when the pattern started to form in early 2011. Even well into 2012, we would not have known what, if any, classical pattern was forming. It was only in late 2012 and early 2013 that we saw that prices were coiling and forming a symmetrical triangle.

While we did not have to check this chart every day, we still had to monitor it on a regular basis, say every several weeks or so. And even such intermittent vigilance is not so easy for those of us, especially beginners, who are not used to systematically going through our charts even when nothing interesting or tradable seems to be developing. Continuous diligence can be burdensome for experienced traders too. We could be single-mindedly and unwisely focused on a potentially explosive set-up or a post-breakout action while ignoring our basic job as classical chartists: to look at charts.

That said, missing this set-up was not a disaster. We may see this chart for the first time only after the breakout. Or we may have been viewing this chart every two weeks or so, but, because we did not draw any preliminary boundaries that framed the price action, we did not spot the coiling triangle. Or perhaps we were busy focused on other compelling set-ups and breakouts. Or, we may get lucky and spot this set-up for the first time just as it is nearing a breakout. My point is that we must accept the fact that we will miss many setups, including giant patterns such as this symmetrical triangle. We are not perfect, and we don't need to be. In fact, we must not pursue perfection given the inherently highly imperfect nature of chart trading, including the necessity of taking many small losses. We find some and we miss some. And even when we miss a breakout, the set-up will often give us second and third chances to enter through retests or continuation patterns.

Let's now look at the daily chart to focus on the breakout:

FIGURE 92

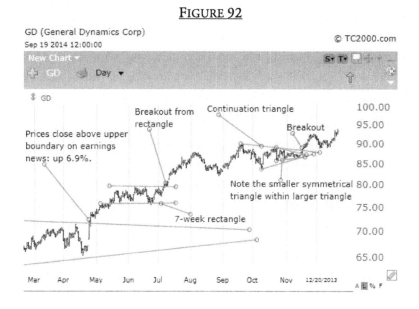

Prices closed above the upper boundary on earnings news. With the immediate volatility of the earnings release out of the way, we could buy shares around the closing price and set our stop just below the breakout day low. We had a good opportunity to buy shares for the next several days as prices did not immediately jump up and force us to risk more than prudent. Then prices gradually increased for the next 3 weeks and the stock was up about 10% since breakout. Everything was going well: clean breakout, good follow-through, and no difficult retest. Then came the challenges. In late May, prices stalled and started to trade in a narrow range. Everytime prices seemed ready to make a run, they would reverse and decline before turning up again before stalling yet again.

This situation captures one of the dilemmas and mental challenges of trading: we have a 10% profit on our position and we want more given the decisiveness of the breakout from a massive textbook pattern, but we also don't want to lose the profit we are sitting on. It is easy to say now that we should just wait patiently, that we should do other things and check back in several weeks to see what happened. If we got stopped out, then so be it. Only in hindsight do we know that prices eventually broke out from this trading range and went higher and higher. Don't get me wrong: we should direct our energy elsewhere after entering a trade. But the reality is that it is difficult to be so detached from a trade given our emotions.

One way to achieve some detachment is to take profits on a portion of our position, say, one-third or so, and let the rest ride the price action. I like this option. It acknowledges our emotions. It also accounts for the possibility that the breakout can fail and prices crash down through the pattern boundary. Still, I think it is a worthy goal to try to stay with our full position until a resolution. After all, we know that if prices decline and we get stopped out, we will suffer a small loss that was accounted for and even expected in exchange for making a worthwhile bet on a compelling breakout.

The choice is ours. We must choose a trading style after considering our personality, capacity for detachment, and preferences. No single trading strategy will produce the best outcome in all scenarios. Instead, we must choose a trading style that suits our temperament and gives us the best chance for long-term success.

Let's return to the General Dynamics chart. Let's assume that we we missed the initial breakout. We were disappointed but it is a mistake to banish a chart to the trash bin out of frustration. Instead, we will revisit this chart as part of our regular cycling through of our stock list. Perhaps in a week or two there will be a retest that brings prices back down to the pattern's upper boundary and create another entry opportunity. Or perhaps a continuation pattern will form and provide a good entry spot.

Two weeks pass and it is early May. Prices are steadily climbing. There is no reason for us to enter and chase. By late May prices seems to be trading in a narrow range. Prices are still trading in a range in the middle of June. We notice that the price dip into early June was reversed at the exact level where a price decline in mid-May was reversed. We now have a potentially significant support level and we draw a horizontal line. If prices close decisively below this support, then we know that a hard retest or even a pattern failure is a possibility. Another possibility is that this support can form the lower boundary of a continuation pattern that pushes prices higher. These are simply possibilities for now and we continue to wait and observe because we have no reason to enter the trade.

Two more weeks pass and now it is late June. We see that our preliminary support level bounced another price dip in mid-June. We also notice that a possible resistance level turned back two breakout attempts in June and so we draw an upper boundary. We now have well-established support and resistance boundaries. Was a rectangle forming? If so, would it be a continuation or reversal rectangle? No need to rush to judgment. We'll wait and observe and enter only if we have a clear price signal and a compelling entry spot.

It is now early July. Prices are making another run to our upper border. This time prices close above the resistance. We have a clear breakout and an attractive reward-to-risk scenario. We buy shares around the closing price of the breakout day and set our stop just below the low. Then we move on and continue to cycle through our charts.

What if we also missed the breakout from this continuation rectangle?

Disappointed, and that's understandable. But we should never despair and never chase. We won't and don't have to catch every pattern and breakout. And new patterns are forming all the time. We need to continue to look at charts to find new set-ups. So we calmly move on and look at the General Dynamics chart five or six times in the next three months as we cycle through our charts. We don't see any patterns developing. The only thing that jolts us is the steady rise in prices that we missed. Again, it is okay to be mildly disappointed but we must control our emotions and never chase. **Berating ourselves over missed trades is completely unnecessary as there will always be more set-ups. We should use our modest disappointment as motivation to be patient and do our homework.** Nobody said consistently trading well would be easy.

Four months pass since the breakout from the continuation rectangle and it is now early November. We notice that prices coiling and forming a possible symmetrical triangle. We draw preliminary boundaries to help us monitor this development. And we put this chart in our urgent folder for regular, perhaps daily, check-ins. A week passes and we see that the price fluctuations have continued to narrow: a symmetrical triangle was definitely a possibility. We also notice that we can draw the possible boundaries of a larger symmetrical triangle that engulfs the smaller triangle: the always interesting pattern-within-a-pattern phenomenon. We monitor daily this chart and see a breakout from the smaller symmetrical triangle on November 14, 2013. We decide to buy shares around the closing price of this breakout and set our stop-loss order just below the low. We are risking just above 1% of our position to enter this intriguing breakout, which may also launch the breakout from the larger symmetrical triangle. Indeed, the next day prices decisively close above the upper boundary of the larger triangle. Buying shares around the closing price of this second breakout still meant risking just 2% of our position.

We have to continue to cycle through our charts and hunt for set-ups in all market conditions. Long-term diligence is just as important when we are on a winning streak. We will grow and, more fundamentally, preserve, our capital only if we continue to trade well, and we can trade well only if we are continuously spotting favorable set-ups. If, instead, we get confident and neglect to do our homework, we will bet on weak setups. Our gains will quickly become large losses and lead us to a destructive cycle of financial loss, frustration, pain, and more loss.

CHAPTER 29

Trading the Market Indexes, and A Lesson in Stubbornness

As traders, we look at individual set-ups. We would not buy the shares of a company at a random spot just because the market is exploding higher. Nor would we short the shares of a company just because the market is declining. However, most stocks move with the overall market. That means we should trade mostly long set-ups in a rising market and mostly short set-ups in a declining market.

So if we find a compelling upside breakout from a textbook classical pattern amid a declining overall market, we may trade this set-up but do so as an exception to the overall declining trend. Edwards & Magee stress the importance of trading mostly in the direction of the overall market and how short trades in a rising market and long trades in a declining market should be undertaken sparely and only as partial insurance against the bulk of our trades being in the same direction as the overall market. Long-term trends do not usually reverse overnight. Trends continue longer than traders and investors expect. Remember, classical chartists seek to participate in, rather than predict or anticipate, the price trends that start from patterns.

There are times when the direction of the overall market and the price action of individual charts give a mixed signal. For example, we may find that the overall market as measured by the major market averages is either trading in a range or in a general uptrend while we see many short set-ups on individual charts. What should we do? The most important rule is to remember that we do not have to do anything. There is no rule requiring us to trade for any reason. I have learned that trading as few times as possible

268

often pays off the best, even when there are some promising set-ups and breakouts. Sitting still and watching and waiting for the most compelling set-ups where the reward-to-risk ratio is overwhelmingly in our favor is perhaps the best way to ensure longevity and profitability in the markets. And nobody prevents us from waiting for these fat pitches ... except ourselves. We will always be our own worst enemy.

Individual charts are prone to false break outs in a choppy market. When the major market indices are trading in a range, I often see breakouts from textbook patterns reverse quickly and lead to pattern failure. Then these formerly-ideal patterns will often evolve into nothing or a different classical pattern. Therefore, I try to trade as little as possible in a range-bound market. If I do trade in a sideways market, I tend to trade only the major market indices using ETFs such as the QQQ (Nasdaq 100), SPY (S&P 500), IWM (Russell 2000), and DIA (Dow Jones Industrial Average). Regardless of how often we trade the indices, we must pay close attention to them as most stocks will move with them most of the time.

Let's see how we could have traded the indices in the first half of 2014.

QQQ: Continuation diamond pattern

While I did not trade it well, this set-up was one of my favorite patterns of 2014 because it reaffirmed the value of classical charting. Let's first get a big-picture view of the situation:

FIGURE 93

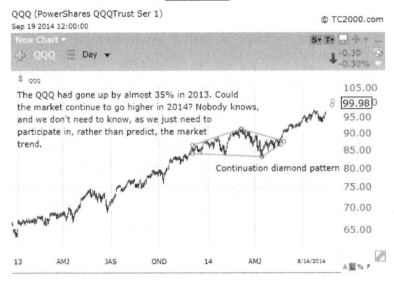

A textbook diamond pattern. Looking at it now, the pattern seems so obvious. It may also seem obvious that it would continue the multi-year uptrend. Surely every trader who was paying even modest attention must have made money on this set-up, yes? That's what I would think too if I saw this chart for the first time months after the pattern had launched a breakout and reached its price target.

But remember that we have trade in real time and not in hindsight. If I sound condescending, then please know that condescension is not my intent. My intention is to warn us that these hindsight judgments are misleading and simply wrong. Again, we trade in real time, and in real time the market was very choppy and imposing great frustration and losses on traders. The perfect boundaries we see now included much volatility and uncertainty. I am not saying that we needed to decode random price movements or get lucky predicting the future to trade this set-up well. To put it bluntly, all we had to do was wait and allow the chart to declare its likely intention. And waiting is what is so difficult for all of us. Much patience and discipline were required to observe the evolution of the chart over several months. Then, just as important, we needed courage and nerve to enter the trade upon breakout.

Let's start in early December of 2013. Here is the QQQ chart from late 2013 onwards:

FIGURE 93.1

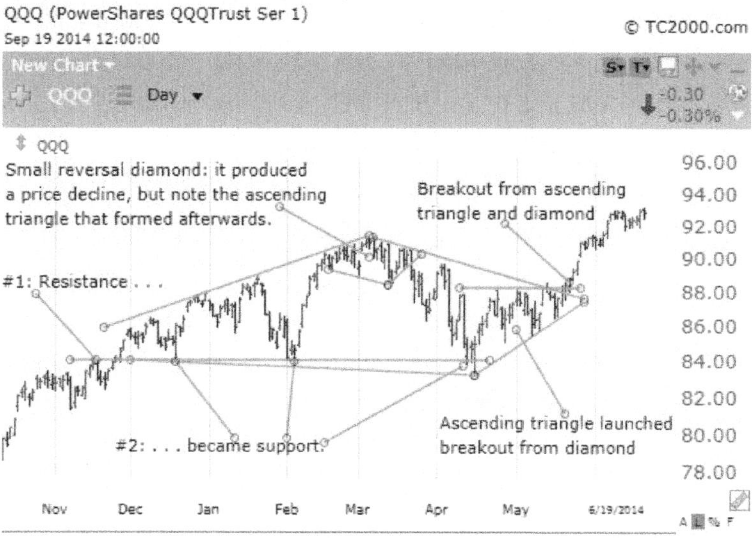

The stock market had been on an incredible run throughout 2013 and it seemed nothing would derail its historic rise. There was some choppiness in December but the QQQ was still up for the month. The QQQ continued to rise through mid-January before suffering a 6% drop into the February low. Then the QQQ reversed and went up for two weeks straight. Prices stalled in early March before declining into the early April lows.

So the market was volatile, but the market is always volatile. Prices sometimes go up and sometimes go down. Amid the ever-present uncertainty, was there a way to make sense of this price action? We will find that returning to the most basic fundamentals of classical charting, and we cannot get more basic than support and resistance, will always be productive and enlightening. Notice that the February and April lows traded but did not close below the support level dating back to November 2013. In fact, prices bounced strongly off of this support.

Another way to help us frame the price action is to always draw preliminary and possible boundaries. Notice that a rising resistance line from December 2013 to March 2014 has about 10 solid touches. Just as intriguing was how a declining support line from December 2013 to the April 2014 low got three solid touches. And there was also the fact that a declining resistance line from the March 2014 highs also had multiple solid touches. Was it possible that a diamond pattern was forming? If so, would it be a continuation or a reversal diamond pattern?

So far we have not discussed whether these price developments presented any trading opportunities. As a classical chartist, we trade decisive breakouts from classical patterns. We might also trade standalone support and resistance levels if they also present a clearly defined and favorable reward-to-risk scenario. Here, we could have traded the bounce off of the support level dating back to November 2013.

What about the possible diamond that was forming? Was there a compelling early entry point for the possible diamond pattern?

I thought there were intriguing developments that suggested, to me at least, that this possible diamond would be a reversal pattern that would start a significant decline in the markets.

First, there was a well-formed mini-diamond pattern that formed at the very top of the possible larger diamond.

Second, there was also a possible horn top that formed soon after the breakdown from the mini-diamond. I looked at the mini diamond and horn top as promising early entry points before a possible breakdown from the diamond. A potential pattern-within-a-pattern is always interesting, and now I thought I was looking at an even more intriguing two smaller patterns within a larger pattern that could start a powerful downtrend.

So I had an opinion and also traded on what I thought were compelling entry opportunities. Having an opinion and trading on logical entry points are not problematic. What is problematic is being so attached to any one possible scenario. And I made this mistake. I was so excited about this multiple-pattern set-up starting a big downtrend that I closed my mind to alternative outcomes. For my multiple-pattern scenario to become reality, the mini-diamond and horn top patterns had to be the catalysts of a significant downtrend and nothing less. I so wanted the chart to play out according to my opinion.

By being so stubborn and inflexible, I was of course ignoring an alternative scenario: that the mini-diamond and horn top could both work by producing modest price declines reflecting their small sizes but that afterwards prices may still break to the upside out of the possible diamond pattern. And the chart offered ample clues that an upside breakout was a real possibility when an ascending triangle seemed to be forming in the last part of this possible diamond pattern. You may be asking why I failed to see this ascending triangle. My answer is that I did see it. But seeing something and accepting it are different things. If I may say so, I think we have a large capacity to ignore reality and instead believe what we want to believe. And I wanted my original opinion, that the diamond would be a reversal pattern, to become reality.

So strong was my bias that I came up with many excuses to justify not changing my mind and buying shares when prices broke out to the upside from both the ascending triangle and the continuation diamond.

Why was I so stubborn? I wanted the multiple-patterns-within-a-pattern scenario to work and not waste the textbook mini-diamond and horn top that had formed. But the reality is that the small topping patterns did work. What also worked was the ascending triangle that formed immediately after these small topping patterns. I was too close-minded to accept the possibility that they were part of the construction and evolution of the continuation diamond pattern.

A trading principle that I have found to be very valuable is that traders should wait until a pattern proves itself. That is, we should not jump to conclusions and predict. Instead, we should simply participate in the trend. There was nothing deceitful about the breakout from the diamond pattern. We had plenty of time to buy shares while risking a very reasonable amount of our position. All we had to do was wait, observe, and let the chart declare its intention. This is why early entries, even based on logical entry points, must be used with care: they can make us inflexible and lead us to miss the real breakout. It is crucial to always have an open mind and consider opposite scenarios, especially when we have entered in anticipation.

It would not be an overstatement to say that the skills needed to successfully trade this breakout from the continuation diamond were the ability to draw lines and to understand the direction of the breakout. Drawing and knowing up from down. We learned to do these things in kindergarten but along the way we also learned how to over think and pursue personal glory.

SPY

Now let's see how the other major stock indices were doing. The major indexes will almost always move together so we would expect the SPY ETF that tracks the S&P 500 index to be in an uptrend in this period as well. And indeed SPY was trending up from May to July 2014:

FIGURE 94

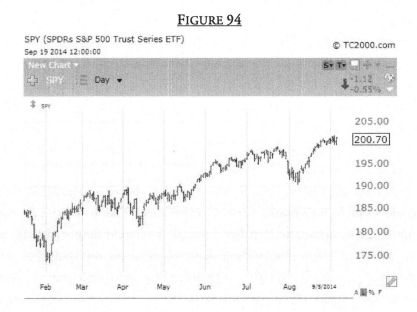

DIA

Let's now look at the DIA ETF that tracks the Dow Jones Industrial Average:

FIGURE 95

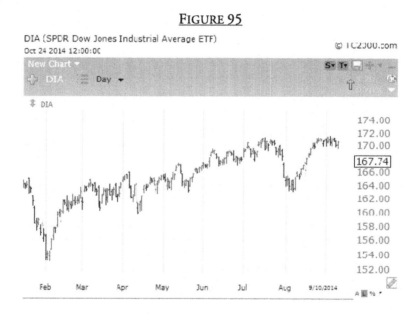

DIA was also in an uptrend from May to July 2014.

SPY vs. DIA: which should we trade?

The stock market was rising during this time and the three ETFs tracking the three major indices all reflected this uptrend. Does that mean we could have used any one of the three ETFs to trade this trend? Remember that we would not buy any stock at a random price just because the overall market is rising. We would look to enter only if there was a compelling set-up with a clearly-defined and favorable reward-to-risk possibility. The diamond pattern and the breakout from it provided a favorable entry spot in QQQ. Was there a well-defined pattern on SPY's chart that provided a compelling entry point? Yes, in the form of a continuation H&S bottom as shown on Figure 96:

FIGURE 96

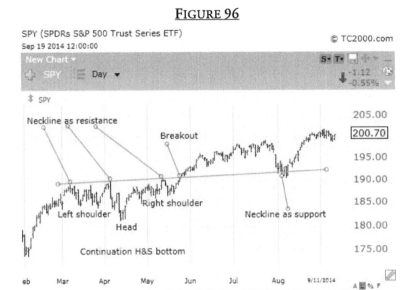

What about DIA: did its chart produce a classical pattern? No, in my opinion, it did not. So while QQQ went up after forming a textbook 5-month continuation diamond and SPY went up after a 2.5 month continuation H&S bottom, DIA simply went up without forming a tradable pattern. This absence doesn't negate the fact that DIA was going up. But from a classical chartist's perspective, that omission meant we did not have a compelling trade on the DIA chart.

There is a saying that it is hard to make money in a rising market. Even the strongest bull markets have periods of declining prices. Investors who buy rising stocks just before the market begins a decline are prone to selling just before the market resumes its uptrend. Patience is still very much necessary even and especially in a raging bull market.

Traders are even more vulnerable to losing money in a bull market. A rising market lulls traders into thinking that making money is easy and they do not have to be careful in choosing chart set-ups. So they start to enter early and make anticipatory trades and hope that a rising market will forgive their haste. The results are large losses, and even more damaging, mental pain and loss of confidence. The frustration of losing money in a bull market is a uniquely painful experience. Our best defense is to be even more patient and careful when trading during a bull market. We have to continue to do our homework and trade only the best set-ups. Big losses are guaranteed the moment we get overconfident.

The fact that most stocks move with the overall market most of the time leads us to a vital implication: we should save most of our financial and mental capital for times when the market is trending strongly. If the overall market is trading in a range, then it is likely that there will be relatively few decisive breakouts from individual charts. Individual stocks will also likely be range-bound and perhaps methodically constructing but not yet breaking out of classical patterns. And there is a higher likelihood that individual breakouts may turn out to be false breakouts that lead to further chart evolution before the real move. Of course there will be individual set-ups that break out and strongly trend even when the overall market is stuck in a range and we should always make trading decisions based on each set-up. But I think it is better to deploy the bulk of our trading capital when the major indices are breaking out of trading ranges and possibly starting a run. Thus, we need to look closely at SPY, QQQ, and DIA to understand what the overall market is doing.

Looking back at my first couple of years of trading, I realize that concentrating my focus and capital to trending periods would have been the single best thing I could have done to dramatically improve my trading results. I would be up 20% to 30% when the market was trending but lose much of it or more during range-bound periods when I got stopped out trade after trade. Instead of stepping back and realizing that the market was choppy and not trending, I would trade increasingly unfavorable set-ups trying to recover my losses. More losses led to more frustration and more chasing of bad set-ups and yet more losses. I had entered the cycle of pain, and I could blame only myself.

We need not fall into this trap. By observing the major indices and having the discipline to wait for trending periods, we can reduce our losses and increase the likelihood that we keep our profits. Time and time again I am struck by how much of trading comes down to patience. If we get only one thing out of this book, I hope we learn that the market will give patient traders many compelling set-ups at some point. The trick is that we do not know when that time will be. But the set-ups will be there. We need patience. Surely the market can demand patience in exchange for giving us the opportunity to learn about ourselves, exercise discipline, and perhaps even make some money.

CHAPTER 30
50-day and 200-day Simple Moving Averages

I use only two indicators: the 50-day and 200-day simple moving averages. I use them as supplemental but not controlling references. These two moving averages are the only visual data displayed on my screen other than price and volume. A good charting program will allow us to display the moving average of our choice. Ask customer support if you need help setting up moving averages on your charts.

Why these two moving averages instead of, say, the 10-day or 100-day or any other period? The 50-day and the 200-day moving averages are some of the most referred to indicators among traders and investors. I have found the 50-day and 200-day averages to be effective support and resistance levels often enough to warrant observation but not be the final determinant of my trading. Prices and breakouts are still the most important factors in my trading decisions. As a trader, I am a chart purist.

Others may feel that different moving averages, say, the 30-day and 100-day, are better secondary reference points.

We have to be cautious, though, when choosing and using moving averages. Just as there is no single entry and exit strategy that will produce the best outcome in every situation, there is no moving average that will always be the ideal reference point for every chart. Because we can display any moving average we wish, the danger is that we choose the moving average that confirms our wishes or "explains" the price action in our favor.

How not to use moving averages

Let's say that we have a breakout from a descending triangle. The lower horizontal boundary is at the $17.50 level. Prices decline to $17 then reverse and the pattern fails. We ask why the price bounced up from the $17 level instead of continuing to go down. We don't see any previous support or resistance levels at $17. The 50-day and 200-day moving averages are nowhere near the price action. So we start charting different moving averages to fit the price action. After trying the 10-day, 13-day, 17-day, and etc., we find that the "35-day" moving average was just under $17. So we conclude that the 35-day moving average formed a support level and was the reason why prices failed to decline farther and the pattern failed and, worse, resolve to buy shares when prices return to the 35-day moving average.

Such tweaking of the moving average to "explain" the price action in hindsight is very misleading and dangerous. We have stopped being disciplined classical chartists trading only decisive breakouts from textbook patterns and instead have started to trade randomly. There is likely no reason other than coincidence why prices reversed at the $17 level and the 35-day moving average happened to be at that level as well.

How moving averages can help

Let's look at an example where the 50-day and 200-day moving averages functioned as powerful resistance. The following chart shows a possible H&S bottom that formed in Mechel Steel Group from February to June 2014:

FIGURE 97

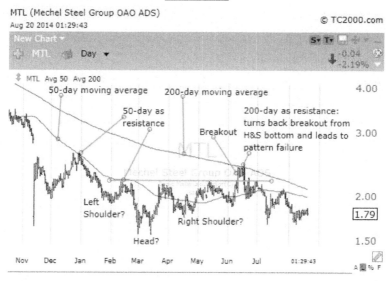

A decisive breakout in early June seemed to confirm the pattern. We notice, though, that the breakout stopped just under the 200-day. Prices then traded in a narrow range for several days. It was possible that prices were forming a bullish flag or pennant that would propel them through the 200-day resistance. Instead, prices quickly reversed after briefly trading above the 200-day and closed decisively below the neckline of the H&S bottom. Prices failed to close above the neckline again and the pattern failed over the next several days.

In my view, the key question is not whether we should buy shares given the fact that the breakout failed to close above the 200-day, but whether there was a compelling entry opportunity after the breakout – the basic and most important question we must ask for every set-up. That the breakout stopped just under the 200-day is an interesting but a secondary concern for me. Whether I enter this trade will depend on whether there was an advantageous entry spot after the breakout, and here there was none. Why? The breakout, despite being stopped by the 200-day, was powerful: up 13.2% on the day. I would not have used a buy-stop order in anticipation of a possible breakout because MTL is a relatively low-volume and high-volatility stock. That meant that I would have to decide whether to buy shares after the powerful surge. And it was clear that I was out of position after the breakout: I did not want to risk more than 13% of even a small position to trade this breakout.

Would I have bought shares if the breakout was more modest, say, rising only 3-4% on the breakout day instead of more than 13%? Yes, because I saw a decisive breakout from a promising pattern despite the fact that the potential resistance of the 200-day was overhead. I trade breakouts from classical patterns and not moving averages. I have found that even when the 50-day and 200-day averages function as effective support or resistance, they only rarely affect my entry and exit plans. In contrast, an upcoming earnings release will always change or halt our trading. If one of these moving averages overlaps a pattern boundary, then we may conclude that the boundary's resistance or support potential may be stronger than otherwise. But this possibility does not significantly affect my trading since we are looking for a decisive breakout through the pattern boundary whether or not the 50-day or 200-day is nearby. A breakout through a key boundary and the 50-day or 200-day makes the breakout more credible. But our trade decision still rests on whether we have a favorable entry spot.

PART III

CONCLUSION

CHAPTER 31
Life and Trading

Nothing can bring you peace but yourself.
Nothing can bring you peace but the triumph of principles.

Ralph Waldo Emerson

As we said at the beginning, trading is speculating. With its lure of quick profits, speculation seems uniquely well equipped to bring out the worst in ourselves. But we simply cannot succeed in trading with a get-rich-quick mentality or any short cut. Trading well means doing our homework, being patient, limiting risk, moving on after setbacks, pursuing diverse interests, living life, and recognizing that our lives are bigger than trading. Again and again. Informed and prudent trading, far from requiring a gambler's lifestyle, is based on a continuous affirmation of worthy values.

Remember that we do not have to prove anything in the markets to anyone. We do not have to trade to secure our financial future. Thrift and living within our means are always available and effective ways to build a solid foundation for ourselves. If we choose to trade, we should do so with discipline and caution, always remembering that protecting our capital, not making money, is our priority. If we apply these truths to our trading, we will find that trading can be a source of wisdom, self-discovery, and yes, even excitement.

I plan to publish a book of instructive and recent chart patterns on a regular basis. I am sure there will be many interesting classical patterns to choose from for the next volume of this book. Some are forming now, some will form later, and some are breaking out as I write these last sentences.

285

The patterns will be there. We must bring the patience, discipline, and perspective.

I wish you the best. Farewell for now.

CHAPTER 32
Suggested Reading

Here are some books that I enjoyed and offer fundamental knowledge on trading, investing, and the financial markets. We should take time to learn before committing our time, energy, and money to the market.

"Technical Analysis of Stock Trends" by Robert D. Edwards & John Magee

I use the 5th edition (1966) for my daily reference. I also have the 4th (1957) edition. The 4th edition is essentially the same as the 5th, but the charts in the 4th are not as clearly drawn as the charts in the 5th. I bought my pre-owned 5th edition from Amazon.

"Technical Analysis and Stock Market Profits" by Richard Schabacker (Harriman House 2005)

While Edwards & Magee deserve praise for their work, they acknowledge Schabacker as the original founder of classical charting. You don't need to buy both Schabacker and Edwards & Magee. Either book will suffice.

"Market Wizards: Interviews with Top Traders" by Jack D. Schwager (Wiley 2012)

Informative and fun interviews with prominent traders. The book is not about specific trading strategies. The value of this book comes from learning timeless principles (e.g., cut your losses quickly) and the importance of the mental game.

"A Random Walk Down Wall Street" by Burton G. Malkiel (W. W. Norton 2003)

A good introduction to the stock market. Malkiel argues that chart traders and fundamental investors' efforts to beat the market are futile. Instead, he urges everyone to use low-cost index funds to invest in the stock market.

Traders must be open to opposing ideas and different possibilities, and this book is as far from classical charting as you can get. If you agree with the message of this book, then you should not trade.

"The Intelligent Investor" by Benjamin Graham (Collins 2006)

A book on picking stocks using the value investing approach. Ironically, one of the main messages of the book is that we should just invest in low-cost index funds rather than pick individual stocks. The book is ultimately a cautionary tale about the stock market. Before we decide to trade or invest, we should learn what we are up against.

ABOUT THE AUTHOR

Brian studied at the University of California at Berkeley and at Harvard Law School. He is a student of economic history and the financial markets. As a Harvard Law School Post-Graduate Research Fellow, Brian researched the relationship between equity returns and national politics. He has authored articles on economic issues in publications such as the *Harvard Journal on Legislation*.

Brian is a writer, investor, trader, and trading coach.

You can follow Brian at portfoliocareerist.blogspot.com and on Twitter: @PortfolioBrian.

Brian can also be reached at brian.b.kim@gmail.com.

DISCLAIMER

Everything in this book is for informational, educational, and entertainment purposes only and is not to be considered professional advice of any kind. All statements and opinions in this book are not meant to be a solicitation or recommendation to buy, sell, or hold securities. Trading and investing involve risk and may result in financial loss. All trading and investment decisions you make are your own.